DEALING WITH DOWNTURNS: STRATEGIES IN UNCERTAIN TIMES

A Convoco Edition

CORINNE MICHAELA FLICK (ED.)

Convoco! Editions

Convoco Foundation
Brienner Strasse 28
D–80333 Munich
www.convoco.co.uk

British Library Cataloguing-in-Publication Data: a catalogue
record for this book is available from the British Library.

Edited by Dr. Corinne Michaela Flick
Translated from German by Philippa Hurd
Layout and typesetting by PressBooks

Printed in Great Britain

ISBN: 978-0-957-295-889

Previously published Convoco titles:

Collective Law-Breaking–A Threat to Liberty (2013)

Who Owns the World's Knowledge? (2012)

*Can't Pay, Won't Pay? Sovereign Debt and the Challenge of Growth
in Europe* (2011)

"In the middle of difficulty lies opportunity"
—Albert Einstein

CONTENTS

INTRODUCTION

Dear Friends of Convoco,

Convoco comes from the Latin *convocare*, meaning "to convene." Since its foundation, Convoco has called for the exchange of knowledge. Convoco is a knowledge network that offers curated content, creating points of reference and connections, and above all encouraging exchange. It brings together individual disciplines, and its activities extend across the areas of science, economics, politics, media, and culture. Antidisciplinary thinking that transcends subject areas offers the best way of managing the complexities and uncertainties of our world today. We are aiming for and creating serendipity. When we confront global problems together we must find new ways of collaborating.

It is inherent in the nature of action that we must deal with both success and failure. They are alternative scenarios in an uncertain future, and only by realistically acknowledging that we have to deal with both of them will we be able to act wisely. This knowledge can be traced back to the context of the military, where strategic thinking was developed. For the first time defeats were anticipated, and suitable courses of action in the case of failure were drawn up. The definition of strategy is knowing suitable courses of action after suffering a defeat, as "fortune favors the prepared mind." In such a competitive world and economy as ours, this means that whoever has the best strategy will win.

The global nature of our environment is subject to continual change and unpredictable influences. Today's challenge is to be able to deal with the resulting uncertainties. It is imperative that we act strategically both on an individual and on a collective level.

Corinne Michaela Flick
January 2014

THESES

CORINNE MICHAELA FLICK

Failure is present as a possibility in any action or venture. In order to fail "well" it is essential to have a strategy, for then one recognizes alternatives and can admit mistakes. Strategies are essential—they can turn a defeat into a victory and create success in the face of adversity and an unfavorable starting point.

CHRISTOPH G. PAULUS

The revelation of the law as a way of controlling the uncertainty of the future.

STEFAN KORIOTH

We expect the law to create regulations applicable even to situations that are characterized by risk and "non-knowing." This can be successful if uncertainty is not seen as a problem or a degenerative phenomenon associated with postmodernism, but as an inevitable and productive part of knowledge. The law contains strategies, from rules regarding the burden of proof to rules governing liability, that can reduce complexity and distribute the social risks of "non-knowing" in an appropriate way.

JENS BECKERT

Failure means falling short of goals of a particular action. However, the problem of uncertainty questions this model of action. If the conditions of the action are not fully known, as there is no complete information available, and the future also cannot be derived probabilistically from the past, how do actors make decisions? One solution would be to act as if it were possible to determine means-end relations unequivocally. An alternative is to understand decisions in quite a different way, that is as a process of trial and error, in which the goals and means of the action adapt again and again to the new experiences that are encountered over the course of the situation. In this way action is understood neither teleologically, as if controlled by a goal that exists outside the process of action, nor traditionally, as if based on unquestioned habits. Rather, it is understood as a continuously situational process of adaptation based on the information to hand. If we are to take uncertainty seriously as a starting point, such a pragmatic model of action is a possible alternative. Failure then becomes a normal part of action, but it can also be seen more clearly as an obvious starting point for processes of learning that form the basis of further decisions.

PAUL KIRCHHOF

Freedom overcomes uncertainty and contains uncertainty within itself. But freedom creates hope out of the unknown, the invisible, and the uncertain. This hope refers to the individual human being, his right to self-determination, his joy in creativity, and his sense of responsibility. Freedom is the principle of the individual who hopes.

BAZON BROCK

Even the extinction of the dinosaurs after a meteor strike and the decline of all empires that have ever existed are not capable of reducing in the least our optimism that we can survive the worst if we learn how to deal with it. These are the words of the prophet of doom who is nevertheless smart enough to survive, as he knows that by changing the descriptions of this awful prospect he can avoid being harnessed to the yoke of doubt and euphoria.

SAUL DAVID

For Carl von Clausewitz, the great 19th-century Prussian military theorist, the role of "strategy" in war was vital. But his definition of strategy was not that used by Sun Tzu nor as military theorists understand it today—in effect, the commander's method of planning and conducting a campaign—but, rather, the use of engagement or battle for the purposes of war: in other words it is the interface between policy (the political aims of war) and tactics (the means of fighting a battle). Clausewitz was convinced that without a firm grasp of strategy—understanding how military operations could achieve policy—no general could hope to be successful.

JÖRG ROCHOLL

The possibility of failure must be *real*, as this creates the strongest incentives for individuals to make decisions assuming full responsibility.

KAI A. KONRAD

"Gambling for resurrection" is among the favorite strategies used in the face of failure by decision-makers, but it is also one of the most dangerous. Someone with their back against the wall can either give up, or enter into a bet. This promises rescue with a certain degree of probability. But there is also a residual probability of a huge amount of damage. One would not take on this bet if one did not need to, as the gain in the event of success is considerably smaller than the loss in the event of failure. The bet is actually a bet on financial loss. But for someone backed against the wall, this bet is attractive. He will profit if he succeeds; and he does not bear the loss himself if the bet is lost. Others will bear the loss, or at least the best part of it.

GERD GIGERENZER

In an uncertain world statistical thinking and the communication of risk is not enough. Good rules of thumb are vitally important for good decisions. A rule of thumb or *heuristic* allows us to make a decision quickly without much searching for information but nevertheless with a high degree of accuracy.

BURKHARD SCHWENKER

It is not change as such that leads to failure, but the inability to recognize change in good time and respond resolutely and courageously.

CHAPTER 1

STRATEGY—A BASIS FOR SUCCESS

CORINNE MICHAELA FLICK

Strategies are essential in order that we may be able to act successfully, as the future is always uncertain. No one can make accurate predictions about what will happen tomorrow. In the course of every venture we must be aware that, under certain circumstances, our ideas and projects cannot be implemented and that different actions from those originally planned might have to be taken. Dealing with the possibility of downturns is part of every enterprise whether in the private, economic, or public sector. This is a fundamental given, and applies particularly in periods of uncertainty. It becomes necessary to act strategically.

That is, the actor needs to have clarified the various scenarios of action possible before he or she begins their enterprise. Even if the starting point is not perfect, strategies can help to offset such a disadvantageous situation. With the right strategy, those starting out under worse conditions can ultimately gain the advantage.

DEALING WITH UNCERTAINTY

Today our world is dominated by uncertainty. That means on the one hand that events occur that could never have been imagined and on the other hand that probabilities of possible outcomes cannot be analysed.[1] One cannot rely on trends and prognoses. Predicting the future has become impossible.[2] Neither politics nor economics can depend on planning systems from the past. Dealing with this uncertainty presents a particular challenge.

The way to limit the uncertainty of the future lies, as the political theorist Hannah Arendt says, in the possibility of making and keeping promises, legally speaking, in the inception and fulfilment of contracts. Thus the law is an essential instrument for limiting uncertainty, but only insofar as the contractual parties adhere to the understandings and agreements that have been made. Even if a breach of contract is sanctioned, this is no guarantee of legal compliance. Legally binding agreements make the future only a bit more predictable. A large degree of residual ambiguity remains, and with it the danger of a project failing.

At the same time, however, uncertainty is also the central condition of capitalist economic activity. It opens up opportunities for innovation and creativity and enables new participants to become established in the market.[3] This is what creates progress and growth. Uncertainty can be seen as a constituent requirement of capitalist economies.[4]

Thus uncertainty has two sides: an increased sense of risk and related feelings of insecurity among players of the market; and at the same time the creative aspect that promotes growth.

DEALING WITH DOWNTURNS

Only the foolish and arrogant do not consider the possibility of defeat. Dealing with downturns—that is with a project going awry—should be part of every life plan, every business idea, and every act of governance.[5]

As Seneca wrote: "His first thought [was] that something might obstruct his plans."[6]

This also reflects the Christian idea of humility. Humility is a condition for a happy life as it protects against hubris. The humble person is also aware that they cannot influence every circumstance. Greek mythology offers numerous examples of how human hubris can bring downfall and death. We need only think of Icarus or Tantalus; the failure to acknowledge that between heaven and earth there exist powers and laws besides one's own leads to destruction. As Schiller's Wallenstein says: "We sow the seed and they [the powers of destiny] the growth determine." Equally, overestimating one's own skills while underestimating those of one's opponent or competitor is a sign of foolishness. We should always be aware that the other person is also capable, perhaps even more capable than oneself.

Even if failure occurs, it does not have to mean the end. A defeat can be the beginning of something new and better. Fundamental to this principle is the notion of the comeback. We should consider failure a kind of learning process. The philosopher Karl Popper showed science how to make discoveries via a failed attempt. He called this method "falsification." Here a scientist sets up hypotheses whose significance is only proven if they cannot be disproven. Science recognizes the principle of "trial and error."

The economist and journalist Tim Harford draws the comparison with evolutionary biology, as evolution is the natural process in which success can start with failure.[7] Biology continually varies hereditary characteristics, adapting the individual to his or her environment and thus enabling the individual to survive in a constantly changing world. If we take Harford's idea a step further we might realize that constant change and adaptation offer the only possibility of protecting oneself from events whose occurrence is not imaginable and which therefore appear completely out of the blue. Continual change and adaptation disempowers any twist of fate.

Behind all this lies the idea that a defeat merely means "it doesn't work like this," and that another attempt under different circumstances can still lead to success. Dealing with a lack of success demands proactive behavior.

This presumes a paradigm shift. Failure must become socially acceptable, and it must not have a stigmatizing effect that makes future action impossible. The community should acknowledge that acting can mean making errors and making errors can mean failing. It is not about whether people fail but how they fail. As Samuel Beckett said: "All of old. Nothing else ever. Ever tried. Ever failed. No matter. Try again.

Fail again. Fail better."[8] What is true of the individual and the community applies to businesses, too: every business should have a no-blame culture, in the sense that it deals openly with mistakes. A business that allows for mistakes to happen has the opportunity to grow as a result of them because it learns from them. Of course there are limits to which mistakes can be acceptable in business.

In order to fail "well" it is essential to have a strategy, for then one recognizes alternatives and can admit mistakes. Strategies are essential in dealing with mistakes. They can turn a defeat into a victory and create success in the face of adversity and an unfavorable starting point.

STRATEGY IS A PLAN FOR DEALING WITH DOWNTURNS AND STILL ACHIEVING ONE'S GOAL

The concept of strategy was developed by the Prussian army when it faced the superior forces of Napoleon's Grande Armée. The Prussian general Carl von Clausewitz developed his theory of strategy while on active service during the Napoleonic Wars. Even today, his famous book, *On War*, forms the basis of many political and economic strategies, and still underpins contemporary thinking among the international armed forces. It combines rational, objective analysis, which has been a focal point since the Enlightenment, with the Romantic tradition that draws on the psychological, emotional, and intuitive elements of our decision-making. In this way the book takes account of the duality of human judgment: "Two souls, alas, dwell in my breast."[9] Clausewitz discusses the calculating and rational side of warfare and its irrational and unpredictable characteristics in equal measure.[10]

Strategy means sounding out possible scenarios for action. Thinking in advance and anticipating various developments and outcomes creates an advantage, namely that the individual is prepared for any possible event that might thwart the desired course of action and the expectation of success, and he or she can act accordingly. A strategy is developed in good times, so it is at hand when things start to go wrong. It is, however, precisely in uncertain times when it is important that strategic thinking and action should not be developed in isolation from reality. In strategic planning external circumstances should always be taken into consideration and reflected in the concept itself.[11] Although strategy is about foresight and planning, it can—and must—be altered again and again to suit external circumstances, even during the venture itself.

However, strategy must not be equated with tactics.[12] The latter describes action within a situation, where it is more expedient to react than to act. Tactical decision-making is fast, while strategic planning is often an ongoing process where everything happens more slowly. Uncertainty must be part of the calculation when strategies are being developed. One cannot, as in tactical decision-making, act on the basis of real circumstances.

As "everything must be conjectured and assumed,"[13] it can easily happen that one's own convictions start to waver and one begins to doubt one's own strategy. Strategic decisions are always trade-offs—decisions made between mutually exclusive alternatives. Which is ultimately the right one is not predictable and often can only be decided with the aid of intuition.

Clausewitz refers to intuition as an important strategic tool when he talks about presence of mind.[14] When dealing with uncertainty the psychologist Gerd Gigerenzer also emphasizes gut instinct. In an uncertain world complex methods of decision-making that make use of information and calculation are often worse, and can cause more damage, than intuitive decisions, because they arouse unfounded hopes of certainty.[15] In this case a strategy that uses emotional intelligence as well as reason can be advantageous.

If we make intuition-led decisions it is essential to act with conviction, and we should pursue an internal plan. Every strategic decision requires strength of will. In order to succeed the individual must be able to endure uncertainty, confusion, and doubt, without feeling the need to search for facts and logic. The poet John Keats called this a person's "negative capability."

Finally, we can conclude that failure is present as a possibility in any action or venture. In order to deal with mistakes and failures it is essential to work with strategies. Strategic thinking does not create certainty with regard to the future, but it prepares us for difficult situations.[16] Planning and foresight, and therefore strategy, are the basis of success, as "Fortune favors the prepared mind."[17]

Notes

1. In situations of risk the probabilities of events happening can be mathematically calculated. But if risk turns into uncertainty this is not possible. In his book *Risk, Uncertainty and Profit,* the economist Frank Knight (1885–1972) makes a similar distinction in differentiating between risk

and uncertainty: for him risk means situations in which actors can match the outcomes of actions with probabilities. By contrast, uncertainty characterizes situations in which such a probability calculation is not possible. Cf. Jens Beckert (Max Planck Institute for the Study of Societies), "Die Abenteuer der Kalkulation. Zur socialen Einbettung ökonomischer Realität," in *Leviathan*, 35 (5) (Berlin: Springer/Verlag für Sozialwissenschaften, 2007), p. 300.

2. "Economic forecasts are often the scientific by-product of economic analyses that are based on a theoretical understanding of economic circumstances. If the findings turn out to be robust and reliable, they can be extrapolated into the future insofar as the causally responsible factors can be considered satisfactory with respect to their future development. [...] In actual experience, however, a comprehensive, conceptual understanding of concrete reality is often lacking. In this case a forecast can be made on the basis of an extensive statistical evaluation of appropriate time series data or system indicators, where the fundamental correlation between the forward looking and already forecast variables are weak or inexistent." Klaus Zimmermann (President of the German Institute for Economic Research), "Warum Prognose die Krise verschärft haben," in *Handelsblatt*, 20 March 2009.

3. "Including uncertainty establishes the indeterminate character of economic decisions because actors cannot fully anticipate the consequences of their actions, and thus it emphasizes that the future is open in principle. The indeterminacy of decisions makes economic situations contingent and thus opens room for creative behavior or entrepreneurial activity." Jens Beckert, *Beyond the Market: The Social Foundations of Economic Efficiency*, trans. Barbara

Harshav (Princeton: Princeton University Press, 2002), p. 38.

4. Cf. Beckert, "Die Abenteuer der Kalkulation, " p. 299.

5. Cf. Bazon Brock in Bazon Brock and Peter Sloterdijk (eds.), *Der Profi-Bürger* (Munich: Fink Verlag, 2011), p. 44.

6. Seneca, *On Tranquility of Mind*. http://thriceholy.net/Texts/Tranquility.html

7. Cf. Tim Harford, *Adapt: Why Success Always Starts with Failure* (London: Little, Brown, 2011), pp. 16–17.

8. Samuel Beckett, *Worstword Ho*, 1983.

9. Johann Wolfgang von Goethe, *Faust*, book one, 1808.

10. Cf. Michael I. Handel (ed.), *Clausewitz and Modern Strategy* (London: Routledge, 1986).

11. "Strategy [...] makes the plans for the separate campaigns, and regulates the combats to be fought in each. As these are all things which to a great extent can only be determined on conjectures, some of which turn out incorrect, while a number of other arrangements pertaining to details cannot be made at all beforehand, it follows, as a matter of course, that strategy must go with the army to the field in order to arrange particulars on the spot, and to make the modifications in the general plan which incessantly become necessary in war. Strategy can therefore never take its hand from the work for a moment. That this however has not been always the view taken, generally, is evident from the former custom of keeping strategy in the cabinet and not with the army ..." Carl von Clausewitz, *On War*, trans. J. J. Graham, Book 3, chapter 1.

12. "...Tactics *is the theory of the use of military forces in combat. Strategy is the theory of the use of combats for the object of the war.*" Clausewitz, *On War*, Book 2, chapter 1.

13. Clausewitz, *On War*, Book 8, chapter 1.

14. Clausewitz, *On War*, Book 1, chapter 7.

15. Gerd Gigerenzer, *Risiko: Wie man die richtigen Entschei-dungen trifft* (Munich: Bertelsmann, 2013), p. 58; and Gerd Gigerenzer, *Risk Savvy: How to Make Good Decisions* (New York: Viking, 2014).

16. "Businesses fail to understand that absolutely no instruments exist that can eliminate the uncertainty of economic action. Thinking strategically does not bring certainty as a consequence, but rather it prepares us for difficult situations." Bolko von Oetinger, "Plädoyer für die Ungewissheit," in *Die Zeit*, September 2003.

17. Louis Pasteur (1822–95).

CHAPTER 2

DEALING WITH DOWNTURNS AS A FUNDAMENTAL HUMAN PROBLEM: THE "INVENTION" OF THE LAW

CHRISTOPH G. PAULUS

Since the notion of "downturn" or "failure" contained in both the title of this essay and in this book denotes a process that is to be understood solely in the context of the passage of time (see below), it is perhaps appropriate that we should agree on this basic concept before we go on to focus on the "invention" of the law.

I.

Failure is a concept that is located on a temporal axis and solely and exclusively understandable in this context insofar as it is necessary to posit a pre-history that has brought about the subsequent failure of events. It presupposes a plan or expectation that has not come to pass in the desired way, with the result that the implicit prognosis of the future differs from actual developments. For those affected, this divergence is called success or failure, according to their point of view and scale of values. Both emotions presuppose differing expectations and are thus linked to what has gone before.

As it lies beyond my professional expertise I shall refer only in passing—but nevertheless draw attention—to this close relationship between success and failure, as here two concepts that at first sight seem antagonistic and oppositional appear in direct proximity. All over the world both individual and collective experiences demonstrate and have demonstrated countless times that what was originally experienced as failure turned out to be a success, and the other way round. The assessment of one and the same event clearly also depends on the period of time that has passed between the beginning of the event and our reflection upon it. But of course it is not dependent on time alone: some failures are—and remain!—a failure over the course of an entire lifetime, and the same applies to success. In this case people with differing characters can develop differing viewpoints: those who feel at home with affliction will give in to failure more willingly than someone who sees good fortune in every situation. Thus we can see that characterizing an event as a failure is a wholly relative concept that cannot always be agreed upon.

The dependence of failure on a previous action or inaction presupposes human knowledge of causal connections and thus touches on the most painful shortcoming in those of our faculties related to human intelligence or our cognitive capabilities, that is being condemned to having no idea of what the future will bring, apart from our existing knowledge of the past and the present based on our concept of time. The depth of this pain is revealed sometimes indirectly, sometimes directly, through various insights and sources of evidence.

Indirect indications include, for example, the production of calendars, a task that been attempted almost all over the world throughout human history. From the Egyptians via Mesopotamia, from the Mayas via the Chinese, from the Celts to Stonehenge observation of both the heavens and the tides in particular has served to map what may happen—that is, the future. From earliest times, mastering this task brought humankind huge increases in prosperity, in particular through the cultivation of river and coastal regions.

Direct evidence includes the ancient craft of fortune-telling that can be found in practically all historically documented cultures. Whether it is taking the auspices, reading the entrails of slaughtered animals, interpreting strange events, casting horo-scopes (the famous astronomer Johannes Kepler, for example, performed this task, among other things, for Wallenstein during the Thirty Years War), or producing extremely complex calculations such as performed by modern rating agencies, all these activ-ities are intended to allay fears of an uncertain future, reveal the unknowable, and thus make it predictable for those who want to know.

II.

Another, indirect example lies more particularly within the professional competence of the present author—although in the first instance the topic still has much to do with speculation. Any knowledge of so-called legal anthropology notwithstanding, we do know that the regulation of life, and thus an early form of the law, begins when Robinson Crusoe teams up with Friday, that is when a community of people is formed, however small. Such an alliance necessarily leads to systems of governance that regulate communal life in some way.

However, we have no idea exactly when the history of human development reached the point when people came to the conclusion that what someone has promised must also be adhered to by that person in a binding way, that is when, legally speaking, something resembling a "contract" was invented. The consequences of this are enormous. Let us look at a common contemporary example: I can demand the delivery of goods I have bought; by contrast I cannot demand to be invited to dinner after the invitation has been withdrawn. At some time the point must have been reached when people said that a promise made is no longer a non-binding statement of intent, but something upon which the recipient of the promise can and should be able to rely.

We can speculate in many ways as to why humankind over the course of its development created this proposition, and why it was accepted by other people. We might be inclined to foreground the common root of the current German word for "contract", *Vertrag,* and the German verb *vertragen,* meaning "to tolerate," and thus to see the contract as an instrument of peace. This idea can be confirmed to a certain extent if we compare the Latin word *pactum*, which is derived from the verb *pacisci*, meaning "to make peace." But we can certainly go beyond this etymology and suggest that a promise understood to be binding was not related to some past events, or to events that are long since over, but to commitments that were to be fulfilled only in the future in some way. For a commitment, or more precisely the "invention" of a binding promise, is unnecessary if we are talking about the past: it makes no sense to state with binding effect that I delivered a bale of straw last month. Commitment is not relevant or essential unless and until is it a question of a future event, and only if this future event means that my earlier delivery of the bale of straw could possibly lead to a dispute.

If we are prepared to pursue this train of thought, the development of the contract (and subsequently of the law as a whole) can be seen to be a comprehensive attempt to control the uncertainty of the future and to make it more predictable. For example, going back to basics, we might look at the German Constitution and its Preamble. Here we can see immediately that in its very nature even this constitutional pillar is nothing other than a way of controlling the ever-present specter of past experiences, at least as far as the future is concerned, by erecting a bulwark against the return of this apparition.

A random selection of further examples clarifies what we mean here:

- Under inheritance law one of the basic questions is how long the so-called "cold hand" (that is the testator) should be allowed to issue instructions and be able to control the life of the so-called "warm hand" (the heir) by means of terms and conditions contained in the will. Under German law there exists in numerous instances a thirty-year limit and thus a restriction to one generation. Under Anglo-American Common Law, by contrast, they have been grappling with the incredibly complicated "rule against perpetuities" for many centuries.

- In family law marriage is similarly a promise for the future; and here, too, the historically minded question of why the legally binding phenomenon of marriage exists globally reveals strategies for controlling the future. It seems likely that marriage as a legally binding bond is only to be understood in the context of the statement that the ancient Romans expressed so pointedly, namely *pater semper incertus*—the father is always uncertain. In order to control this biologically institutionalized uncertainty regarding the male sex, the legal union of marriage still offers the most reliable guarantee of the unambiguous parental assignment of a child born to a married woman.

- Criminal law imposes a criminal penalty on all kinds of activities in order to control future behavior thereby. But even if one does not want to regard punitive aims, which have been argued over for literally millennia, as future-oriented (whether individually or generally preventative), but rather as a retroactive atonement for past actions, in terms of the legal reaction to this the educative (and therefore future-facing) component at the very least exists intrinsically in order to set an example. The same can be said in civil law of any sanctioning of particular actions by means of an obligation to pay compensation.

In short, the law as a whole can be seen to be a human construct that attempts to direct people's innate uncertainty about the future in a preordained fashion, and thus to give it at least some kind of structure. In this way potential failure becomes the subject of actual defense strategies.

III.

For those who find the aforementioned thoughts, notions, and ideas far too speculative and therefore dubious, we might offer another example of their (at least apparent) veracity. The essence of this particular contemporary example lies in the fact that one specific process in life is not yet codified in law, and for this reason every time it recurs it unleashes a shock wave of risk and helplessness. We are talking here about sovereign bankruptcy, a phenomenon with a centuries-old history whose latest incarnation in Greece is even today—almost four years later—still not finally over.

It is as surprising as it is disturbing that this phenomenon of a state declaring bankruptcy, irrespective of its unerringly regular reappearance (the Spanish King Philip II "succeeded" in having to declare his country bankrupt three times during over forty years on the throne, and a relatively conservative list of bankruptcies over the last 200 years remarkably records over 270 cases), has still not been contained by the aforementioned model of the regulation of future threats, uncertainties, and situations that need to be controlled. As a result each new occurrence of sovereign bankruptcy leads to a frantic search for solutions, each time beginning again from scratch.

This process of starting from scratch has always been about the decision-makers trying to gain time and thereby (and herein lies the irony of this attitude) driving up the costs of an ultimate solution (which, moreover, is frequently never found) on the one hand, and increasing the misery of their citizens on the other. This statement is by no means a simple reflection or projection of what has recently taken place in Greece. Rather, it is a pattern that recurs consistently all over the world. Argentina's sovereign bankruptcy of 2001 is still fresh in our memories; but there are many cases where the poor and the poorest states on earth regularly "succeed" in going bankrupt (repeatedly) and do not receive any publicity from today's media. In these cases, however, bankruptcy filters through with much more immediate effect on each country's citizens, with the result that hardship and death are consequences that are experienced on a mass scale.

By contrast, if there were a predetermined procedure, ex-ante uncertainty would be if not averted then surely managed in an orderly fashion. For Eurozone members this orderly process should, according to the marketing, begin with the European Stability

Mechanism (ESM). But a closer inspection of the agreement reveals that the ESM is merely an institution that functions as a receptacle, as it were, within which politicians continue acting and making decisions as they have done before (in particular during the Greek crisis).

This initial feeling of helplessness is not being averted by the ESM. This could only happen if a procedure with fixed rules were to be set in train. There are several suggestions for this: the International Monetary Fund's (IMF) Executive Board brought them all together for the first time in a report of spring 2013. Almost all these suggestions agree that a neutral authority should take control and work alongside a restructuring of the national economy in question, both with regard to the country's debts and in terms of the economic structure of the nation.

Only with the establishment of such a system could uncertainty regarding the future be contained within a structure, but only insofar as it is clear ex-ante to the decision-makers what steps must be taken. Various signs indicate that within the Eurozone at least the time is more than ripe to introduce such a procedure. Then, and only then, could we avert the failure of politics that we have seen recurring time and again.

CHAPTER 3

LAW, KNOWLEDGE, AND UNCERTAINTY: A SKETCH

STEFAN KORIOTH

I.

All procedures and activities, all important actions and communications within the law and a particular legal framework, determine and process information and knowledge.[1] Reconstructing and describing the facts, searching for the appropriate legal norm for the relevant legal questions, interpreting and understanding legislation, seeking out and processing court judgments through which it can be assessed how the courts might or will decide on a particular legal dispute with any probability—all these procedures are dependent on the basic operation of handling information and knowledge. The same applies to the creation of new laws by establishing regulatory objectives and the means to be used in unilateral legal transactions, in contracts, and in regulations and laws. Language, and in the modern legal system this means the written form of language that makes everything readable,[2] is an essential instrument in doing this. The unilateral supply of knowledge, as well as discussion, judicial dialogue, interrogation, controversial debate about individual statements whether they are normative or on points of fact, are the usual procedures. Legislation, documents, libraries, indices, archives, and databases are typical means of making these processes possible, documenting them, and making them available to the parties concerned, third parties, and the general public. "Knowledge is omnipresent—more of it than one can know. Every single activity presupposes knowledge. For every action and for every communication knowledge is indispensable."[3] The relationship between knowledge and language refers to the limits of the possibilities opened up by this relationship. Thus, just as the limits of my language describe the limits of my world, the legal world and its limits are described through what is captured by language.

II.

This is where "non-knowing"[4] makes an entry. First of all, this is quite normal in various legal phenomena and in the operation of the law. Non-knowing can concern the past in the form of non-knowledge or ignorance of facts, and should then typically be converted into knowledge, or at least belief that this had been the case. The judge in a criminal court should explain the facts on which the charges are based using the means that the criminal procedure makes available. He must be convinced of what has happened, and whether a criminal charge is justified or not. If this is not possible, the constitutional rule is invoked whereby doubts, which are above all doubts about knowledge, are taken into account in favor of the defendant. First and foremost, however, the law also formulates a behavioral expectation that is oriented towards the future. Whoever signs a contract or enacts a law wants to mold the uncertain future in a normative way and make it as predictable as possible. No one can guarantee that this will succeed. No "is" follows from the legal "ought," either in the present or in the future. In the future the law can be infringed, and events can develop in unpredictable ways such that neither contracts nor laws can comprehend them or manage new problems appropriately. That, too, is an everyday occurrence that legal routine in the forward-looking form of contracts and norms includes in the broadest possible form. Contracts can contain safeguard clauses, adjustment provisions, or termination options; laws can be changed, be of limited duration, or include experimentation clauses. Here the art of the lawyer is needed to recognize possible future developments, evaluate their probability, and make provisions that will make the uncertain future as predictable as possible.

The normal, everyday kind of non-knowing also includes non-knowledge of the law, the legal position which can be dealt with by bringing in suitable expertise. In this situation, too, the law offers numerous regulations. In criminal law, for example, a clause dating from ancient times still pertains, saying that ignorance of penal prohibition does not in principle protect one from punishment. Many people who are ignorant of the behavioral requirements in the case of a traffic incident and who incur a penalty for failing to stop after such an event—the criminal law talks of illegally leaving the scene of an accident—may have had bitter experience of this.

Alongside these familiar instances of non-knowledge there is something that can be described as specific non-knowledge, namely the uncertainty, the non-knowledge that cannot be eliminated at all or not in the foreseeable future, but that must nevertheless be dealt with. At the moment we do not know what dangers might emanate, for example, from the use of nanotechnology or genetically modified foodstuffs. We do not know what the authorization or non-authorization of pre-implantation genetic diagnosis (PGD) might mean. Nevertheless the law is required to come up with regulations for dealing with such possible opportunities and dangers regarding new developments and technologies. In addition we sometimes cannot know whether the current factual basis for legal decisions is in any way commensurate to the problem, and what effects certain regulations will create (by this I do not mean non-observation of the law but, rather, the consequences of the law actually being observed). If, for example, the uncertainty surrounding the complex relationships between the international financial crisis and the sovereign debt crisis could be eliminated, concepts concerning the legal aspect of managing these crises could be devised (which, of course, might not exclude the possibility of several plausible courses of action). But instead of this there are many, and an increasing number of areas of uncertainty, all the way up to the now proverbial concept of "unknown unknowns." The most recent sociological studies, in particular, are instructive about the reasons for this. It is not only a question of the advancement of the natural sciences and technology. This advancement creates risks—which differ from uncertainty in that the probabilities of certain consequences happening are quantifiable—and uncertainties as a necessary side effect of new knowledge. There are also very tangible social reasons for this increase in uncertainty that are crucial for the organization of society. There is an increasing disintegration and fragmentation of social institutions, and of the certainty and security of established patterns of behavior and rituals—the Church, the family, associations, social strata, systems of protection that guarantee security in society are all affected, but equally the world of work and individuals' working lives are touched by the most diverse forms of pluralization. All this increases the individual's possibilities of action and choice on the one hand, while on the other it is a source of insecurity and isolation that is linked cognitively with uncertainty.

Taking action today frequently means taking action in uncertain circumstances.

For its part modern science has distanced itself from the idea of the linear expansion of available knowledge for a long time now. The optimism of the Enlightenment, where humanity's questions were increasingly managed and resolved efficiently through the use of the intellect, and the belief in the controllability of the world through knowledge and intellect have not just been shaken up, they are consigned to the past—whether once and for all remains to be seen.

Scientific studies tell us that the proliferation of knowledge today primarily increases ignorance, above all, however, that each specific domain of knowledge is becoming increasingly isolated from the other, and that knowledge can mean risk while ignorance, by contrast, contains possibilities. To this extent today's fashionable expression the "knowledge society" is a euphemism—according to Ulrich Beck the world risk society is a non-knowledge society in which the increase in knowledge in itself leads to an acknowledgment of non-knowing.[5] Nevertheless, if the desire for knowledge, now as always, represents one of the strongest drives in human society, it is because this describes a fundamental, positive anthropological state of human belief and hope, and the desire for knowledge "creates a certain amount of orientational security."[6] In addition, knowledge, and in particular knowledge from which others can or may be excluded, is still power—power over nature, over institutions, or other people, applicable to both stasis and change, to symmetries and asymmetries in knowledge distribution within human society. Finally, there are areas of life whose functioning can only be ensured by uncertainty. If competition is to function in a market, then the observation and decision-making processes of the players must not only be independent of one another. There must also be uncertainty with regard to the reaction of the other market players. In the age of transparency and the possibility of exploiting a person's whole life through digital data by robbing them of their privacy, non-knowing and uncertainty can also be the elixir of life: "I live on what others do not know about me."[7]

III.

Law and jurisprudence are in many respects conservative. Even if its job is to provide a structure that over-arches the future in a normative way, a legal system is not an exclusively rational construct or the result of the simple, deliberate decision by a group or society.

Rather, it is above all a way of storing the experiences of the past that is not available in any ad hoc form but that is fundamentally the product of the particular history and culture of each country (or union of states). Jurisprudence, although it is the oldest hermeneutically amenable textual science and the oldest social science alongside theology, does not need to be at the cutting edge of developments in the humanities and social sciences with its philosophy of science. Jurisprudence is inclined to integrate the findings of other disciplines—economic sciences, social sciences, history, philosophy, philology, theology— into its own systems selectively if they seem productive (and are generally agreed upon within the professional discourse). Most importantly, however, it is frowned upon in all major legal cultures to lose sight completely of the practical application of jurisprudence.

Under these general conditions discourse in jurisprudence is currently taking account of research in the social sciences and philosophy regarding the conditions underpinning knowledge and ignorance, risk, and uncertainty. The question is how must the law—both legislation and its implementation—react to the increase in uncertainty outside and within the legal system?

In the first instance we must understand uncertainty neither as a problem across the board, as a negative phenomenon, nor perhaps even as a phenomenon of the degeneration of postmodernity. Those who talk of "crazy times," meaning an increasing complexity and uncertainty in the way the economic, social, and political systems work, should realize that on the one hand this is no universal finding, and that earlier uncertainties have indeed been resolved; and on the other hand the fragmentation and pluralization of systems does not simply mean just a loss of certainty, but, rather, that they open up new possibilities. Uncertainty raises the possibility of a separation of powers in cognitive and control terms[8]—what must be avoided is the formation of extraneous hierarchies in these fragmented areas of society. In the case of the law, for example, this means that the previous orientation towards ideas of system and balance lose their importance in favor of the creation of mechanisms that support adaptability. Democratic forms of participation and decision-making, for example, must be structured in such a way that social adaptation guarantees the possibility and necessity of continual self-transformation. In this scenario it can be crucial to preserve uncertainty. Insofar as it means acting strategically, politics must be able to include the arcana of uncertainty. This also explains why the illegal acquisition of politically sensitive facts, whether ultimately via the tapping of digital technology, is so dangerous. The procedural aspect of the law becomes more important: if uncertainty is not to lead to deadlock, rules must be found which explain how to proceed in the case of the kind of uncertainty that assists in decision-making. This can mean rules regarding the burden of proof, rules on statements, and on presumptions, but also, for example when dealing with risky new technology, rules governing liability that extend to include absolute liability without fault and that can be linked to compulsory insurance. Ultimately types of behavior with uncertain consequences can also simply be prohibited. In this and other approaches we can see a strategy that is typical of the law: complexity is reduced, courses of action are opened up and closed down, and at the same time they are linked as far as possible to responsibility in order to distribute the social risks of uncertainty as appropriately as possible. Such off-loading strategies can ensure that the basic task of the law is to stabilize and guarantee behavioral expectations, and to make courses of action and legal institutions available even when circumstances change. In this context uncertainty becomes less of a threat, and more of an "opportunity." Failing to address this, however, means that "even a perfect knowledge infrastructure cannot resolve the fundamental problem of uncertainty. Thus from the start legal regulation cannot rely on security, but must institutionalize procedures that in turn make it possible to react to changes in knowledge bases."[9]

Notes

1. Information is about communication; knowledge means a body of findings that can be presumed to be known in each context where the knowledge is used. Thomas Vesting, "Die Bedeutung von Information und Kommunikation für die verwaltungsrechtliche Systembildung," in Wolfgang Hoffmann-Riem, Eberhard Schmidt-Aßmann, and Andreas Voßkuhle (eds.), *Grundlagen des Verwaltungsrechts*, vol. II, 2nd edn., 2012, §20, para. 1ff.

2. Rainer Maria Kiesow, *Alphabet des Rechts* (Frankfurt: Fischer, 2004), p. 35: "Lawyers must be able to read. Ever since the old *Digests* that Justinian had compiled turned up again in the West in the 11th century, [...] writing and reading about the law has proliferated."

3. Niklas Luhmann, *Die Wissenschaft der Gesellschaft* (Frankfurt: Suhrkamp, 1990), p. 146.

4. "Non-knowing" refers to Ulrich's Beck concept of *Nichtwissen*, as opposed to "knowledge" (*Wissen*) as

described in Ulrich Beck, *World At Risk*, trans. Cieran Cronin (Cambridge: Polity, 2009), chapter 7.

5. Ulrich Beck, *World At Risk*, trans. Cieran Cronin (Cambridge: Polity, 2009), p. 115.

6. Wolfgang Hoffmann-Riem, "Wissen als Risiko—Unwissen als Chance," in Ino Augsberg (ed.), *Ungewissheit als Chance* (Tübingen: Mohr Siebeck, 2009), pp. 17ff., 22.

7. Peter Handke, *Am Felsenfenster morgens* (Munich: DTV, 1998), p. 336.

8. Also in this context, an increase in information and knowledge does not necessarily lead to better decisions. See Gerd Gigerenzer, *Gut Feelings: The Intelligence of the Unconscious* (New York: Penguin, 2008).

9. Hans-Heinrich Trute, "Wissenschaft und Technik," in Josef Isensee and Paul Kirchhof (eds.), *Handbuch des deutschen Staatsrechts*, vol. IV, 3rd edn., 2006, §88, para. 40.

CHAPTER 4

THE UNCERTAINTY OF MODERNITY

JENS BECKERT

Failure is only possible if you have a goal. Talking about failure only makes sense as the definition of a gap between what is desired and what has actually been achieved. To this extent failure is the result of a process of action comprised of various components. In this, alongside an actor capable of performing an action, we have the goals of the action, the normative and material conditions of the action, the available means, and the efforts of the actor to reach the goal.[1] If we follow Alfred Schütz's model of action, then even before starting to act the actor imagines the result of the action and acts in the expectation that his doing will lead to the desired result.[2] In his imagination the actor projects himself into the kind of world to which his action should lead. In principle this intentionality of action obtains whether we are talking about companies' investment decisions, a political party's electoral campaign strategy, or debates around the family dinner table.

At the same time we are very familiar with the experience of not reaching our imagined goals. An estimated 50 to 90% of all innovations fail, almost half of all marriages end up in the divorce courts, and career plans often do not bear fruit. Actions are risky in the sense that their outcome is uncertain. The reasons for the discrepancy between the intention of action as expressed in the initial decision and the result of the action are numerous. First, the goal of action cannot be achieved because we miscalculated, we were not in possession of important information, or we interpreted it wrongly. The factors of influence were in principle recognizable, but some of them were simply overlooked or wrongly evaluated by the actor. Second, actions can fail, because certain factors of influence could not be recognized as they did not in fact exist. In this context, against the backdrop of the risks associated with the Iraq War, the former US Defense Secretary Donald Rumsfeld talked about "unknown unknowns." We do not even know what we should be looking for, possibly because this information only arises in an unknown future situation. Furthermore, actions can also fail because of unintended consequences. The desired goal may well be achieved, but so much collateral damage is incurred in the process that one can hardly talk about achieving one's goal any more. Achieving the goal can also fail because of the actor's lack of ability. All the information is available, but the actor lacks the talent, assertiveness, staying power, or self-control needed to achieve the goal of the action. Finally, our goals can change. Even though we have reached our original goal, we experience the result as a failure, as we recognize, on reaching the goal, that (now) we actually want something completely different. Actors' preferences are not stable.

In this essay I will look primarily at the first two of these causes of an action's failure, that is (a) mistakes made when evaluating a situation, and (b) the simple lack of information about the conditions of action that influence how the action proceeds but that are unknown at the time the decision is taken. Both are completely normal in situations of action that arise from trivial decisions. Ultimately it is the complexity of the situation of action that leads to a lack of clarity about the means of action, the conditions of action, and also to the effects of interaction that occur between the actions of a plurality of actors.

Incomplete information leads to decisions that are tainted with the risk of uncertainty. Risk and uncertainty can be examined at the level of the actors themselves and also at the macro level of society. I will look at both levels. Since the 1970s there has existed a distinctive social discourse about the increasing complexity of society and the development of a "risk society." But are we living today in an age that is much more uncertain than before? And if this is the case, what are the appropriate decision-making and organizational models needed to deal with this complexity?

1. RISK AND UNCERTAINTY

Since the 1950s the complexity of the situation of action as a cause of disappointment has been one of the most controversial problems in decision theory. How can optimal decisions be reached if the parameters that influence the results of action are not completely known? At the organizational level there is the question of which decision-making rules permit the consequences of a "normal failure" to remain acceptable to the organization in spite of events. At the level of society taking account of complexity creates doubts about whether societies and economies can be managed by means of political and economic decisions. The consequences of applying levers cannot be predicted and unintended consequences are often the outcome.

An important distinction in the investigation of complex decision-making situations was introduced as early as the 1920s by the Chicago School economist Frank Knight.[3] In his book *Risk, Uncertainty, and Profit*, he distinguished between the two categories of risk and uncertainty. In both cases it is a question of forecasting future events. He defines as risky those decisions that can be placed in a class of comparable events about which past information is available, and whose possibility of occurring can thus be estimated in probabilistic terms. For Knight, decisions are uncertain if they are unique in character and thus their probability cannot be articulated. To recognize how far-reaching Knight considered the category of uncertainty to be, we need merely to see that he put companies' investment decisions, for example, in this category. The immediate consequence of uncertainty is that in a given situation the optimal action is simply unknown. Thus we cannot understand the action of the actors as a rational weighing-up of options among a complete set of all possible alternatives for action.

This raises the empirical question of how actors who want to achieve their goal actually make decisions. According to Knight, entrepreneurs and managers do not act merely on the basis of rational means–end calculations which, in conditions of uncertainty, are simply not possible. Rather, they act on the basis of opinions, evaluations, and intuitions which help them to reach the conclusion that a particular decision is the right one.[4] This does not exclude the use of calculation and the collection of as much information as possible. But ultimately the decision cannot be derived from these data simply in the sense of a solution to a mathematical equation. Rather, decision-makers must interpret the situation; however, they can make mistakes. Contrary to initial appearances, Knight does not consider uncertainty to be bad in principle as he believes that only the uncertainty of a situation of action produces the possibility of profits in business. Entrepreneurs exploit uncertain situations of action. Uncertainty has a positive significance, as without it there would be no motivation to go into business, and because uncertainty is the basis of creativity.

We can identify at least two sources of uncertainty that are in principle different. We can distinguish between the material dimension and the social dimension of uncertainty.[5] By material dimension we mean that particular developments relevant to the situation are unknown. For example, in the case of innovations, of course we do not know what technology is being developed at the start of the process. To this extent we cannot predict whether investment in the innovation will pay off. The social dimension relates to the action of other actors whose decisions are certainly relevant for the outcome of the action, but which are at the same time unknown. Models in game theory address this problem, imputing rationality to the actors as well as complete knowledge of the preferences of the other actors. In real decision-making situations, however, such conditions do not obtain, and as a result the strategic action of one actor is largely contingent as far as the others are concerned. Success or failure can only be understood within the social context of the unpredictable action of other actors.

In economic debates the category of uncertainty plays a major role, for example in the work of Keynes, in economic sociology, institutional economics, and in the work of the Austrian School. For Keynes,

uncertainty can be responsible for a lack of investment, thus justifying state intervention.[6] In economic
sociology and institutional economics uncertainty is
cited in the context of institutions, power, and
cultural frameworks and networks.[7] In Austrian
School economics, uncertainty is the main rationale
for organizing the economy as a market economy.
Any kind of central economic planning necessarily
fails due to the planners' lack of information.

In organization theory, too, uncertainty has been
a frequent topic of debate since the 1950s. Herbert
Simon, for example, was convinced that actors can
only process actually available information in a totally
inadequate way and because of this they call time on
information-gathering if they think they are able to
reach a satisfactory (but not optimal!) decision.[8]
Actors are rational beings only to a certain extent,
as knowledge about the consequences of action is
incomplete, future events cannot be predicted, and
not all decision-making options can be weighed up
one against the other. The environment of the organization is thus regarded by organization theorists as
increasingly turbulent, which essentially means that
the actors have to deal with complex decision-making
situations that are characterized by uncertainty.

2. RISK SOCIETY

Complexity and uncertainty as causes of failure with regard to actions first became major topics in economic theory and in decision theory and organization theory. But since the 1970s the subjects of complexity, uncertainty, and risk have played an increasingly important role at the level of politics and society as well. While the 1970s saw discussions of the consequences of complexity for the political planning process, since the 1980s questions of technological risk have occupied a central position in public debate. The background for this change in the importance of risk and uncertainty in political perception is formed by contemporary experiences above all. By comparison with the first half of the 20th century the postwar era in the West had been characterized by a high degree of political and economic stability, and by the claim that it was now possible to control economic and social processes. The dominance of Keynesian macroeconomic management in all western countries, alongside political programs such as the Great Society in the USA, expressed the contemporary conviction that economic and social developments could be controlled politically. During the 1970s this self-confidence by and large disappeared. The economic and political crises of the early

1970s highlighted more and more sharply the complexity and risk inherent in social and political processes. Direct political control now seemed increasingly improbable. In the social sciences there emerged a debate, still ongoing today, about the risk and crisis inherent in the processes of social development.[9]

This started in the 1970s with theories of ungovernability, as put forward by Daniel Bell, James O'Connor, and also by Jürgen Habermas, for example.[10] In the 1980s this was followed by diagnoses of a risk society and reflexive modernization, by which social theorists referred both to serious ecological risks and to general processes of change in the development of modern societies.[11] In light of this, risk and uncertainty are central to the individual's experience of action in modern societies. Since the Club of Rome's 1972 report *The Limits to Growth*, ecological risks have been widely discussed in social policy. The nuclear reactor disasters at Three Mile Island (1979) and Chernobyl (1986) raised awareness about the risks associated with technology. These risks are still addressed in public debate today, particularly in the debate about climate change, where effective intervention is failing precisely because of a lack of possibilities in the global management of environmental policy and a supposed conflict of interests between growth and environmental protection. Almost no one today believes that these problems can be solved through political control.

The experience of uncertainty and risk exists today in the context of the development of modern society. Anthony Giddens in particular has shown that the concept of risk arises in the first place in the context of the emergence of modern society and society's concept of an open future.[12] Traditional societies do not regard the future as an open space that can be shaped, but as the cyclical return of familiar events from the past.[13] This is connected to the way these societies are characterized profoundly by natural cycles, that is the regular return of the seasons that determine economic activities and shape a mythological world view. Of course even people in traditional societies had the experience of unfulfilled expectations. The future held unpredictable dangers that come about as a result of natural events in particular, such as droughts, floods, earthquakes, or epidemics. But these events are experienced as inevitabilities of fate that people sought to influence through religious and superstitious means should the need arise. These events were certainly not attributed to individual shortcomings. To this extent, one did not talk about failure.

By contrast, risk is categorically related to decisions intended to shape the future, but whose outcome is unpredictable because of the complexity of causal relationships and innovation. The future is neither the circular repetition of what has already been, nor simply the linear continuation of already existing trends. In such situations the actors are not aware of the risk and will probably not be aware of it before it is too late. Only the adventurer who advances into uncharted waters in the hope of finding longed-for riches without knowing what awaits him on the way, and sometimes even without knowing whether there is any kind of goal at the end, for example, takes risks in the modern sense. In modern society the future has become a counterfactual realm of possibilities whose actual shape is contingent upon and influenced by the actions taken by actors in the present. This is a new aspect of modern societies. They have become risk societies in the sense that the future has become a space to be shaped by means of goals. Actors can fail to shape the future by wrongly evaluating possibilities and threats. Unlike in traditional societies this failure is put down to the actions of the actors themselves, and not to fate.

In the process of modernization risks are also created by a breakdown in the forms of integration typical of pre-modern societies. Pre-modern societies base their social integration primarily on family, religion, tradition, and local community.[14] In family relationships one can usually rely on those concerned keeping to the obligations they have agreed upon, independent of considerations of individual interest. Strategic uncertainty is kept low. Second, integration of action is promoted by the geographically narrow context of action within the local community. The relatively low mobility contributes to the actors' "ontological security." Third, religious cosmologies provide "moral and practical interpretations of personal and social life, as well as of the natural world."[15] The options for action for all actors are regulated by religious instructions so that each individual can reliably anticipate others' reactions to their own action. Ultimately tradition is a means of structuring the future whereby models of action proven in the past are perpetuated. Tradition is closely linked to routine and habit and is thus also a means of reducing uncertainty.

The structuring of action by the family, religion, tradition, and locality restricts actors' possibilities of regarding the future as contingent. The options are narrowly limited. The structures in place prevent risk being brought into focus. In the world of economics, for example, social structures prevent the propagation of collaborative economic relationships organized over wide geographic zones along with the associated demanding and risk-engendering processes of cooperation and exchange. If property rights are linked to religious cosmologies, economic action is oriented towards traditions, and family relationships regulate possible relationships of cooperation and exchange, restrictions in economic development emerge that only disappear with the evolution of modernity. However this happens only by paying the price of risk.

The evolution of modern economic structures is linked to the rolling back of tradition, family, religion, and locality. At the same time, action thus becomes considerably more contingent and more risky. In this context specifically modern institutions develop by which risks are in turn limited, and the danger of an action failing or the extent of the consequences of such a failure is reduced. Insurance is one obvious example of this. The first forms of insurance arose in the context of maritime trade, with its temptations of fabulous gains alongside the threat of losing everything. The risk of getting involved in an enterprise with an uncertain outcome became predictable through the enterprise's insurability. It is not merely a historical coincidence that the calculation of probability developed during the early phase of modernity in the 17th century, that is at the same time society became more interested in gambling.[16]

Insurance, statistics, calculation of probability, and regulation are responses to more and more risky contexts of action in society that enable the stabilization of modern societies' institutionalized risk structures. Without institutional structures regulating them or actuarial calculations, modern financial markets would be inconceivable. Credit agreements need both institutions that can carry out risk assessments of the debtor and also an effective constitutional state through which claims can be met in an emergency. Labor markets are another example of institutionalized risk structures in modern societies. Actors must enter into risks that can lead them to fail. In democratic societies labor markets only become acceptable when insurance mechanisms are also institutionalized to protect against the risks brought about by illness, unemployment, accidents, and old age. The sources of failure are thus transferred from the individual to expert systems. In a crisis it is not just the individual investor who fails, but the very architecture of the financial system. The individual pensioner does not fail, but, rather, the whole pension scheme.

3. MORE RISK?

These new man-made risks make the discussion of a risk society all the more plausible.[17] But can we talk unequivocally about an increase in uncertainty? The development is to say the least ambivalent, as modern society was able to curb many of the dangers that dominated large tracts of human history, dangers that to a great extent created risk. The danger of dying in childhood, losing one's life as a result of an infectious disease, starvation, or being a murder victim has today been dramatically reduced at least in the developed world of the northern hemisphere. Modern societies have reduced many dangers that have thus ceased to be risk factors. At the same time the modern world is characterized by new risks that appear first of all as a result of technical progress. The risk of a nuclear accident is just as modern as that of being electrocuted or being the victim of a car accident. But here, too, institutional structures such as insurance, constitutional procedures, and regulations on risk reduction have at the same time lessened these new risks, or, rather, distributed them among a larger group. If the extent of risk is perceived to be bigger today, however, this could also be due to cultural factors as well as real changes.

At the level of real changes, we can clearly see an increase in the complexity of social organizations. This is a long-term process that has been evolving since the Early Modern period. However, over the last forty years we have seen developments that have increased uncertainty for actors, at least by comparison with the previous postwar period. The interdependency and volatility of economic life have risen considerably due to processes of globalization. The spread of competition and, for example, the global organization of value chains and commercial outlets increase risk for enterprises and make environments seem more turbulent. Rapid change, demands on flexibility, and a general trend towards "social acceleration" make the stability of the future seem less assured.[18] Here the risks are altogether unequally distributed. But overall there arises a social dynamic that is more competitive and exposes the actors to a greater degree of insecurity. One reaction to a future that is felt to be unsafe is processes of social exclusion. The segregation of residential areas, the increase in homophilic relationships in society, and the defense of social privileges in the school system are also expressions of such exclusion processes, by which beneficial social positions are defended against an environment that is perceived to be insecure. In a democratic society these tendencies need to be closely monitored.

But it is also a question of cultural changes. The increase in individualization gives actors an increasingly wide range of options to choose from. In questions of career choice, lifestyle, and living environment the social specifications are much less clearly defined than they were fifty years ago. The same applies to businesses. We are correct to welcome this as an advance in freedom. The flipside of risk is spaces of action that are made available to individuals and organizations. But at the same time modern society expects individuals to see themselves as responsible for their own success and failure within the chosen options. If negative events are interpreted as fate that befalls the actor independent of his own action, the actor does not fail. By contrast, insofar as events in modern societies are to a greater extent attributed to individuals as results of their own decisions, the world seems like a much riskier place, and failure appears omnipresent. The danger of failure is thus also a question of society's prevailing cognitive orientation. The complexity and unpredictability of the consequences of actions can lead to insecurity for individuals and excessive demands being placed on them. Being permanently confronted with options is a continual challenge to identity. For businesses such an excessive demand can arise through the reduction in forecasts and long-term planning. Organizations react to a more complex environment by creating structures and differentiation.[19] Structures, expectations, and strategies exclude the vast majority of courses of action, and thus reduce complexity. Decision-making programs should be set up in such a way that the organization can survive even though individual projects fail.

4. CONCLUSION

I shall return once again to the start of my discussion. Actions, as I have said, are usually understood under the categories of goals of the action, conditions of the action, and the means. Failure means falling short of these goals. However, the problem of uncertainty questions this model of action. If the conditions of the action are not fully known, as there is no complete information available, and the future also cannot be derived probabilistically from the past, how do actors make decisions? Which model of action theory is appropriate to such situations?

One solution would be to act as if it were possible to determine means–end relations unequivocally. Using more and more complex theoretical models and forecasting methods we can attempt at least to come close to the ideal of the perfect, rational decision. An alternative is to understand decisions in quite a different way, that is as a process of trial and error, in which the goals and means of the action adapt again and again to the new experiences that are encountered over the course of the situation.[20] In this way action is understood neither teleologically, as if controlled by a goal that exists outside the process of action; nor traditionally, as if based on unquestioned habits. Rather, it is understood as a continuously situational process of adaptation based on the information to hand. If we are to take uncertainty seriously as a starting point, such a pragmatic model of action is a possible alternative. Failure then becomes a normal part of action, but it can also be seen more clearly as an obvious starting point for processes of learning that form the basis of further decisions.

Notes

1. Talcott Parsons, *The Structure of Social Action. A Study in Social Theory with Special Reference to a Group of Recent European Writers* (Glencoe: Free Press, 1949 [1937]).

2. Alfred Schütz, *Collected Papers* I: *The Problem of Social Reality* (The Hague: Martinus Nijhoff, 1962).

3. Frank H. Knight, *Risk, Uncertainty, and Profit* (Mineola, NY: Dover Publications, 2006 [1921]).

4. Knight, *Risk*, pp. 226ff.

5. Niklas Luhmann, *Social Systems*, trans. John Bednarz with Dirk Baecker (Stanford: Stanford University Press, 1995).

6. John Maynard Keynes, *The General Theory of Employment, Interest, and Money* (London: MacMillan, 1964 [1936]).

7. Jens Beckert, "Was ist soziologisch an der Wirtschaftssoziologie? Ungewißheit und die Einbettung wirtschaftlichen Handelns," in *Zeitschrift für Soziologie*, 25, 1996, pp. 125–46; Douglass North, *Institutions, Institutional Change, and Economic Performance* (Cambridge: Cambridge University Press, 1990).

8. Herbert Simon, *Models of Man* (New York: Wiley, 1957).

9. Ariane Leendertz, "The Age of Complexity. How the 1970s Changed Our View of the World." Lecture given at Max Planck Institute for the Study of Societies, Cologne, November 21, 2013.

10. Daniel Bell, *The Cultural Contradictions of Capitalism* (New York: Basic Books, 1976); James O'Connor, *The Fiscal Crisis of the State* (Basingstoke: Palgrave Macmillan, 1973); Jürgen Habermas, *Legitimation Crisis*, trans. Thomas McCarthy (New York: Basic Books, 1975).

11. Ulrich Beck, *Risk Society: Towards a New Modernity* (London: Sage, 1992); Anthony Giddens, *The Consequences of Modernity* (Cambridge: Polity, 1990).

12. Anthony Giddens, *Risk. Second BBC Reith Lecture*, 1999. BBC Online Network. http://news.bbc.co.uk/hi/english/static/events/reith_99/week2/lecture2.htm

13. Reinhart Koselleck, *Futures Past: On the Semantics of Historical Time*, trans. Keith Tribe (New York: Columbia University Press, 2004).

14. Giddens, *Consequences*, pp. 100ff.

15. Giddens, *Consequences*, p. 103.

16. Jürgen Kocka, *Geschichte des Kapitalismus* (Munich: C. H. Beck, 2013); Giddens, *Consequences.*

17. Beck, *Risk Society.*

18. Hartmut Rosa, *Social Acceleration: A New Theory of Modernity*, trans. Jonathan Trejo-Mathys (New York: Columbia University Press, 2013).

19. Luhmann, *Social Systems.*

20. Hans Joas, *The Creativity of Action*, trans. Jeremy Gaines and Paul Keast (Cambridge: Polity, 1996).

CHAPTER 5

FREEDOM: HOW TO DEAL WITH UNCERTAINTY

PAUL KIRCHHOF

I. THE WILL TO IMPROVE

The individual can remember past events and base his experiences on them; he can observe and make judgments about present events; but he cannot predict the future. He does not know what decisions people will make tomorrow, what mishaps will occur, what inventions there will be, and what lives will be embarked upon. Anyone wanting to predict tomorrow's football results, the stock market indices of the day after tomorrow, or economic growth over the next year will fail. The law has two fundamental instruments for bringing consistency, reliability, and confidence into people's lives. By means of rules—or "pre-scriptions"—the law is tasked with creating the future out of the experiences of the past. It does this using tested, traditional values, and using knowledge about people, their needs, and their character, in order to regulate the future and set binding standards in anticipation of forthcoming, as yet unknown demands made upon the law. The legislator is state power concerned with people's futures.

The second way of dealing with the uncertainty of the future resides in the law's principle of freedom. Freedom means that the individual decides his own affairs himself, personally taking on both the opportunities that come his way and also taking the risks of making the wrong decisions. The uncertainty of the future is made tolerable when the individual takes responsibility for shaping his own life. Of all the decisions concerning freedom, those based on one's own sense of responsibility promise the maximum amount of reliability in terms of the individual, as well as peace in the broadest sense, cultural development, and economic prosperity.

In Greek mythology Prometheus encountered people who still had the ability to predict the future.

Being able to foresee the future also meant they knew exactly when they would die. This affected them profoundly, and they became lethargic. Debates no longer took place on the market square. Economic life weakened. Art and science withered away. Family life deteriorated. When Prometheus saw the people in such distress, he took away their ability to predict the future, thus giving them hope.

This myth tells us a lot about people and humanity. The driving force behind human activity is hope—when we get married, start a family, found a business, build a house, begin a course of study, or develop a research project. People's basic instinct is the will to improve.

II. UNCERTAINTY AS A CONDITION OF FREEDOM

The idea of "freedom" advances our understanding of the law. The law demarcates the individual's spheres of activity and his freedoms, and it regulates a human community in which everyone has rights, powers to act, and responsibilities. Animals that live according to their instincts do not need laws, but if you want to create peace among human beings you make laws. Anyone who wants to ensure that laws are binding in perpetuity emphasizes freedom.

Today, however, some scientists, and neurobiologists in particular, claim that the individual has no free will, and is subject to causal laws of nature that determine his every decision. They say that unconscious forces in the brain control the individual's consciousness, his will, and his actions. According to this theory the individual is not rationally and responsibly in control of himself, but rather—like a skier on a ski lift—he is operated by mechanical forces and led inevitably toward an end point.

If this theory were correct, there would be no freedom, but also no uncertainty. All events would be determined by causal laws of nature, human instincts, or divine predestination. An individual's efforts to improve his life chances through education, performance, and responsibility would be pointless. Responsibilities—blame and liability—would not exist. The difference between good and evil would have to be replaced by the causal categories of cause and effect that come into play without the will and responsibility of the individual. Individuals no longer know anything about care, consideration, love, nor about the common good and public responsibility, nor about the peace created by law, nor about justice—neither the scales nor the sword of justice. Driven by causality each individual seeks the pleasure of the moment, the delusion perhaps that he can somehow gain advantage for himself through his own action.

Our experience argues in favor of freedom. We experience freedom when we decide if we are going to have a glass of wine or a beer this evening, when we carefully consider which book we are going to read tomorrow, and when the day after we make arrangements with our friends to spend the weekend in the mountains or at the lake. We like being determined by desire, curiosity, and the need for relaxation. However, we reserve the right to decide where and with whom we choose the lifestyles that result from this.

The natural sciences alone cannot explain the human individual. Of course his activities are dependent on environmental conditions, on established customs, and on social, legal, and financial conditions. But his intellectual debate covers the choice between duty and inclination, the search for what is subjectively considered more respectable, weighing up alternatives, sifting through and organizing options for action, striving for the new, the contrary, the adventurous, and the unconventional. Art and science, love and enthusiasm, disappointment and sadness, courage and anxiety cannot be explained causally through the natural sciences. Anyone who has looked his own child in the eyes, read a great novel, heard a concert, or made a scientific discovery is immune to any idea of restricting the individual to the causality of the natural sciences alone. And the law requires personal responsibility, blame, liability, atonement, and forgiveness. A society without law would mean a struggle of all against all, the destruction of those in need of protection, and chaos. Thus, even the natural scientist, who believes in the mechanical, naturalistic determinacy of the individual, would have to demand a legal system that protects responsibilities, respects self-determination, and defines blame and liability.

III. FREEDOM IS THE RIGHT TO BE DIFFERENT

Freedom means being allowed to be different from other people. One person spends all day and all night drawing up balance sheets and becomes rich in money; another spends all day and all night writing verses and becomes rich in poems. As people and in their living conditions they are both different, and they will cultivate this difference more as their lives go on. This freedom to be different from others creates a plan out of the general uncertainty of the future, a plan that is desired by the individual and for which he takes responsibility. The progress of one's own life is not tolerated with resignation but shaped according to the personal hopes of the free citizen. The individual knows that his future depends on himself, that it corresponds to his needs and value choices, and that he can coordinate it again and again to suit new situations and realities. The individual cannot deliberately eliminate his finite nature, his intellectual and physical limitations, nor his being bound in space, time, and culture; but he can use this space to explore his creativity in freedom within the constraints of his circumstances and his times.

The intellectual foundations of our culture of freedom have their roots in Christianity, humanism, and the Enlightenment. Christianity teaches that man was created in the image of God, thus establishing the most radical law of freedom and equality in legal history. In this life, each person is given value, endowed with freedom, and aware of their responsibility. Legal claims arise from these attributes. They are inherent to each person, handed down, and thus universal. Humanism tries to combine the educational values of ancient civilizations with the Christian view of the world, and develops standards to shape the life of the individual more humanely according to the model of Greco-Roman antiquity, and to help the individual personality to flourish. The Enlightenment made the law of freedom the basis of human society. The freedom that had been established by nature subjectively within each person is transformed by the law into a freedom that is guaranteed by the state, a freedom that seeks universally established standards.

Thus the modern world is characterized by an idea of freedom that does not accept and tolerate an uncertain future but that shapes it through the self-determination of the individual and his sense of responsibility. The law cannot eliminate uncertainties from human life, but uses them full of hope in light of freedom

IV. CIVIL LIBERTIES

France's *Declaration of the Rights of Man and of the Citizen* (1789) recognizes freedom as the right of each individual to be allowed to do anything that does not harm others. Every individual may exercise his natural rights and freedoms without limits with the exception of those that safeguard the enjoyment of these same rights by other members of society. The law must make these limits clear; it may only forbid activities that harm society.

In the first instance freedom means freedom *from* something. The state had to protect its citizens from three enemies: ill-intentioned citizens, who are silenced by legislation and the administration of justice; individual officials, the authorities, and the state apparatus in general, whose despotism can be eliminated by means of a good constitution; and the enemy from outside, against whose attacks the army acts as a defense. The individual is threatened by his fellow individuals, state authority, and foreign powers, but can expect security through the efforts of all those who concede to each individual his rights. The individual lays claim to a universal law, equality before this law, and security and protection in a community based on freedom.

However, if the individual lacks the material conditions needed for self-determination, he demands the freedom *to* do or have something. He demands property, a job, social security to cover crisis situations, education and training, and above all state provision to protect his life and health. The question of the extent to which the state can create and guarantee the conditions of freedom lies at the heart of the debate about what is the correct economic system.

Ultimately, after securing the freedom of the individual and other associated freedoms, political freedoms become the focus of the community. The individual who wants freedom realizes his freedom in something. In the context of society he claims freedom of speech, of assembly, of association, of the press and radio, and in a democracy he demands participation in elections and ballots. In these different aspects of the idea and concerns of freedom we can see the fundamental choices concerning the extent to which the uncertainties and risks inherent to life can be planned and managed freely by the individual; and to what extent the individual can expect the state to provide both minimum and maximum degrees of security.

V. UNCERTAINTIES—CIVIL LIBERTIES

Freedom liberates the individual, allowing him the self-determined development of his talents, his aspirations, and his concept of community. The more civil liberties are successful in this notion of creating the individual, the more new questions are asked about the principle of freedom, and the idea of freedom becomes uncertain once again.

Freedom in science and technology has led to an industrial upheaval that removes essential production processes from human control and transfers them to the machine—the computer and the robot. Today cars, computers, and pharmaceuticals are manufactured by machines. Man invents and uses the machine; he supervises it and enjoys its products. He is liberated from heavy physical labor. But he is also faced with the question of who owns the results of mechanical production. Traditionally man owned what he produced with his own hands, what he added to nature through his work (Locke). Today it is the machine that produces, creating new goods and values that cannot be found in nature. If we expect the profit produced by the machine to belong to the investor who finances the machine, and who has thus made mechanical production possible, then the reason why this kind of property came about is only called into question at the moment when all the machines' basic productions processes have been completed, and in so doing a huge redistribution of income from manpower to financial power has been effected.

The excess in financial resources lies behind today's developments on the financial market. Here more money is available than is needed for the production of goods and services. And so the market begins exchanging money for money, hoping for changes in value, and betting on the rise and fall of companies and countries. This financial market becomes ever more anonymous, and scarcely takes responsibility any more for the capital investment from which it realizes its returns. It threatens the idea of property that has been gained responsibly and is only therefore justifiable.

Freedom in the world of science creates dramatic possibilities in communication, media, the digital world, and in medicine. Today, if medicine can produce whole genome sequencing quickly and at a reasonable cost, so that one individual can know more about the identity of another individual than the individual does himself, and the one individual is also prepared to change this identity for medical reasons—perhaps also for reasons of regulation and education—then a basic legal concept is questioned: the inviolability of a person's value in terms of his individuality and personality.

Freedom strives for limitlessness and has in many ways—in science, media, on the global economic market, in sport, and in travel—overcome the boundaries of states and continents. There are encounters between countries, legal systems clash, states and the free citizen must come to terms with foreign laws. But this issue does not lie in the problematic lack of a global state, but in the necessity of the separation of powers between many states. State power can only do justice to the citizen if the state thinks and acts like a citizen, if it does not try to force the multiplicity of cultures into an almost uniform world culture, if the condition of democracy—a population that knows its own identity—remains a reality. The importance of the plurality of the almost 200 states on this earth becomes particularly relevant to the individual who wants to escape the power of the regime that is currently determining his life. He can emigrate, immigrate, and seek asylum. If there were only one world state that, according to statistical probability, would probably look more like a dictatorship than a democracy, then such a state could seek out this individual in any corner of the world. He would inevitably be delivered up to this regime.

Freedom overcomes uncertainty and contains uncertainty within itself. But freedom creates hope out of the unknown, the invisible, and the uncertain. This hope refers to the individual human being, his right to self-determination, his joy in creativity, and his sense of responsibility. Freedom is the principle of the individual who hopes.

CHAPTER 6

ANTICIPATION—ONLY RADICAL PESSIMISM GIVES RISE TO WELL-FOUNDED OPTIMISM

BAZON BROCK

As we oscillate between hopes and fears, wishing for success and terrorized by the idea of failure—such are our fundamental attitudes toward the future—we seldom recognize that the representation of situations has a considerable impact on our evaluation of the facts, nor do we recognize how this happens.

The realization that the way a problem is formulated already prejudices our understanding of it was developed by visual artists in the 15th century using the device *ut pictura poesis*. Contrary to common belief this was not merely a question of positively re-evaluating the image of painters, graphic artists, and sculptors, who, up until that point, had been considered mere craftsmen. The question of the recognition of craft — "hand-work" — as an intellectual pursuit — "brain-work," to be included among the *septem artes liberales*, was not about the status of the people involved, as the craft guilds were highly respected. Rather, the notion of *ut pictura poesis* took account of the increasing demands placed upon cooperative planning within the various crafts and on the preliminary work needed to calculate their projects' feasibility. Fundamental to this was the idea of making it easier for customers to make decisions about projects by presenting them with visual options or realizing the project in the literal sense. In short, the necessary move toward working with models in different scales forced the recognition that the ways in which they are represented exert a decisive influence on how projects are defined. This meant that the teaching of proportion and perspective had to be developed. In the Gothic era, whose uniform sense of scale meant that a reliquary would be designed using the same dimensional schematic diagram as a cathedral, major projects ceased to be authorized once the secular authorities no longer felt any commitment to the story of Christian redemption.

Today popular interpretations of *ut pictura poesis* take it to mean that artists, too, are research scientists, and scientists, now that they all work with electronic visualization techniques, must acquire specifically artistic skills. Anyone seriously considering applications for the financial support of "art as research" would have to redefine completely the idea of research. And anyone exploring the level of representation in computer simulations in the (natural) sciences can clearly see that they surpass the majority of artistic presentations. For this reason artists increasingly avoid the representational practices of scientists; and scientists, to enhance their acceptance among the public, allow high-profile interpretations of their visual simulations that are almost on a par with artists' flights of the imagination.

Where this ideologizing of science as art through imaging processes can lead has recently been demonstrated. It was claimed that Galileo, by making drawings of the "moon," the subject of his research, made more profound discoveries than he could have achieved as a mere natural philosopher. These works of art attributed to Galileo were proved to be forgeries. However, the fact that the Galileo drawings could be used as a revelation of the truth of the saying *ut pictura poesis* at all, demonstrates to what extent the "iconic turn" has already become a scientific ideology.

Ut pictura poesis has been part of the ideology of marketing for 120 years, ever since advertising had merely to replace a product review with an enthusiastic representation of the product. A similar example in the contemporary print media is how arts pages reviews are replaced by advertisements for events and reports of art auction sales fetching prices that run into millions. On the stock exchanges the precedence of psychology over economic facts is commonplace, and in daily political life, when justifying one's excuses for having failed at the elections, it is accepted that one has "done a bad job of selling" one's policies, or the appearance of the policy representative has been stage-managed in an unsatisfactory way.

When imagining the future between hope and fear, both artists and scientists have made propaganda out of images that completely mask how the context of fear and hope is determined by evolution. Models of the end of the world are placed in opposition to permanent images of home and an ideal world. To enhance people's convictions to the extent of overwhelming the public, makers of disaster movies and other doomsday visionaries employ the entire repertoire of scientific projections. But simulation techniques were not developed to do this, as "theories of everything ending" exclude any further scientific investigation because it is meaningless. Even the horrific visions of total "ABC war" (atomic, biological, chemical) could not play with the termination of everything, as the calculations revealed that somewhere, in a galaxy far, far away, a few people would survive the fury of annihilation. And both Russian and American generals found it completely unacceptable that, to prove they were the highest form of intelligence in evolution, they should wipe themselves out while a few primitive examples of the human race survived. Up against such tried and tested limits of vanity even the assumptions made about the future by Reagan's US Secretary of the Interior James G. Watt were shelved. Watt had implied that good Christians should look forward to the end of the world as the Kingdom of God could only come into being after such an event.

For reasons of brevity we will not offer any more three-dimensional examples of the unrelated opposition between doomsday visions and millennial or eternal hopes for world peace. The ability to anticipate what lies behind all such speculations teaches us that one must learn to fear in order to be able to hope with any prospect of success. Anticipation describes the crucial characteristic of consciousness in all those systems of living things that rely on learning as a survival strategy. We can thus talk meaningfully about consciousness if the anticipation of attributable events, as results of action as much as natural challenges, leads to the avoidance or de-activation of the dangers we anticipated. In this regard, research based on well-founded assumptions is being undertaken today on the relationship between genetic and epigenetic predispositions.

Even in today's training methods for high-performance athletes the apocalyptically named "look to the end," as it was once known in Christian terminology, is used productively as an encouragement to bear it in mind, rather than surrender oneself to it. Extreme athletes of all kinds can only become active when they have learned to deal with even the most minimal threat to their prospects of success. For example, the racing car driver or downhill skier must imprint and memorize the course in his mind many hundreds of times in anticipation of the demands he is making on himself as an athlete, if he is to give himself the slightest chance of surviving the race by relying on his abilities and skills. Significant successes in the systematic development of the power of anticipation in the realm of high-performance sport to date are the techniques through which tennis players learn to deal with their opponent's return even though the latter has not yet played the shot. With tennis balls reaching speeds of more than one hundred kilometers per hour only such anticipatory abilities can guarantee the continuation of the game.

As for today's customary demands on the ability to anticipate in the context of healthcare, sustainable economic management, and provision for the future, as well as in the context of the overall "problem-solving competencies" of experts, of particular relevance is the element that even power-hungry individuals claim to have recognized as the basis of their effectiveness: the confidence of their target groups. Against all evidence to the contrary, the latter assume that such individuals actually use their anticipatory capabilities exclusively to avoid the dangers they claim to understand well. When a major German bank argues that its employees acted for reasons of passion and not for financial gain, it loses its customers' confidence even if it were established that this passion did not lead to the intention to gain power or was used for financial gain. As is well known, people go for broke because of passion—they also hate and even kill for the same reason. Murder as a crime of passion arouses great interest in the narratives of experimental sociology as such stories play out in the millions of detective novels that are consumed each day. In the crime novel as in the judicial system, in corporate communications as in the political media, etc., iconographies have been established that can only fulfill their function to the extent that they remain constant and at the same time still seem to keep up with the huge changes of conditions taking place in, for example, technical and social developments.

We can learn from the history of the *ut pictura poesis* formula that young people can certainly appreciate collections of historical paintings, for example, even though they completely lack the Christian and theological assumptions needed to decipher the iconography. They replace the external subject matter with intrinsic constructions of meaning as a plausible context for messages. As not only the multiplicity of messages on offer increases with the general availability of representational media, but equally the pressure to make a choice and reach some meaningfulness of contexts, the relationship changes from a demand for constancy to a simultaneous demand for permanent adjustment to change to a fundamental constellation of evidence-based meaningfulness in every different message context.

Such permanent metaphorization in the change of register can be seen in the arts in the genres of caricature, parody, satire, burlesque, grotesque, pataphysics, Dada, and Surrealistic and nonsense literature. In the case of the protagonists of this type of control through Deconstruction, confidence in system-specific iconographies only returns when they prove their strength by disproving themselves through the aforementioned forms of Deconstruction; when they prove their obviousness through the critique of obviousness, and their credibility through doubt; and when they prove that they are controlled by prejudice through the revelation of their prejudices, interests, and self-contradiction. The judge who reveals his prejudices against certain types of behavior—precisely those being displayed before the court—inspires confidence; the judge who says he is only bound by the law is considered a victim of unenlightened self-deception.

Of course the most radical pessimism in the face of the judicial system based on the saying "on the high seas and in court we are all in the hands of divine capriciousness" will not lead to a well-founded optimism about the outcome of the process. The capriciousness of the gods and of nature, random constellations, or the Furies of historic demise and madness, the withdrawal from autonomy through illness or a foreign power are chaotic magnitudes in concrete manifestations of the thermo-dynamic principle. There is no cure for this, but in general we have no fear of the indisputable view that even when our solar system comes to an end all scientific, artistic, cultural, and theological speculation will dissolve into stardust. Even the extinction of the dinosaurs after a meteor strike and the decline of all empires that have ever existed are not capable of reducing in the least our optimism that we can survive the worst if we learn how to deal with it. These are the words of the prophet of doom who is nevertheless smart enough to survive, as he knows that by changing the descriptions of this awful prospect he can avoid being harnessed to the yoke of doubt and euphoria.

CHAPTER 7

CLAUSEWITZ AND STRATEGY

SAUL DAVID

Around the fifth century BCE, a successful Chinese general called Sun Tzu wrote what became a classic manual of military (and latterly business) strategy, *The Art of War*. It is, in effect, a handbook on how to defeat one's opponent in war, and includes such useful tips as "Win all without fighting," "Avoid strength and strike weakness," "Deception and foreknowledge," "Speed is the essence of war," "Bring the enemy to the field of battle (and don't be brought there by him)," and the art of command is for generals to display the "qualities of wisdom, sincerity, humanity, courage, and strictness." Adherents who are said to have put

Sun Tzu's strategic principles into practice include Mao Zedong, General Giap, and the US General Norman Schwarzkopf who used deception, speed, and a strike at the enemy's weak point to defeat the Iraqis in 1991.

Yet *The Art of War* says little about the nature of conflict and its interaction with policy or politics, beyond the fact that "war is a matter of vital importance to the State [...] the road to survival and ruin" and that it is "mandatory that it be thoroughly studied." It was left instead to a 19th-century Prussian officer and military theorist, Carl von Clausewitz, to compile a more comprehensive (but sadly unfinished) account of war—both its role in human affairs and how to fight it—titled *Vom Kriege* [*On War*]. For Clausewitz, the role of "strategy" was vital. But his definition of strategy was not that meant by Sun Tzu nor as military theorists understand it today—in effect, the commander's method of planning and conducting a campaign—but rather the use of engagement or battle for the purposes of war (a concept we refer to today as "grand strategy"): in other words it is the interface between policy (the political aims of war) and tactics (the means of fighting a battle). It was, in his opinion, where the art of the military commander lay and became the central and unifying theme of *On*

War. Clausewitz was convinced that without a firm grasp of strategy—understanding how military operations could achieve policy—no general could hope to be successful.

Clausewitz's overall definition of war is instructive: "War is nothing but a duel on an extensive scale [...] an act of violence intended to compel our opponent to fulfill our will." It is, in his view, a reciprocal relationship that has a dynamic all of its own. Understanding this is vital if we are to judge when and how to go to war.

Since the first publication of *On War* in 1832, however, many commentators have extracted "truths" from it without appreciating two fundamentals: it was a work in progress and contains many apparent contradictions that are, in fact, simply part of the dialectical process; and it needs to be read as a whole, with particular emphasis on the last section, Book Eight, titled "Plan of War."

The most egregious recent misinterpretation—with serious consequences—was by US soldiers and statesmen. In 1975, Vietnam veteran Colonel Colin Powell (the future Chairman of the US Joint Chiefs of Staff) entered the National War College in Washington. While there he read *On War*, later describing the work as "like a beam of light from the past, still illuminating present-day military quandaries."

Those quandaries for him were chiefly the disintegration in Vietnam of the army he loved, and the gap that had opened up between the military and society. In *On War* he found explanations for what had gone wrong. "Clausewitz's greatest lesson for my profession," wrote Powell, "was that the soldier for all his patriotism, valor, and skill, forms just one leg in a triad. Without all three legs engaged, the military, the government and the people, the enterprise cannot stand."

As the military historian Hew Strachan pointed out in a 2007 article for *The American Interest*, "Powell may have been right about the Vietnam War, but he was wrong on Clausewitz." He had misread the final section of the opening chapter of *On War* when Clausewitz describes war as a "strange trinity". Its three essential elements were for him not the people, the army, and the government, but rather passion, chance, and reason. Clausewitz does, it is true, go on to associate passion more particularly with the people, chance with the commander and his army, and reason with the political direction of the government. But in so doing he moved from the trinity itself—which Clausewitz likens to three magnets that are alternately attracting and rejecting each other—to its application. The people, the army, and the government are elements of the state, but not of war, and the distinction is crucial to the relevance of *On War* today.

Powell was not the only American soldier to use Clausewitz to explain what had gone wrong in Vietnam. In 1982, Army Colonel Harry Summers published a paper he had prepared for the US Army War College called *On Strategy: A Critical Analysis of the Vietnam War*. In it he not only repeated Powell's error about the Clausewitzian "trinity" referring to the people, the army, and the government; but he also applied *On War* to identify the missing link in US strategy in South Asia: "The failure to address the question of 'how' to use military means to achieve a political end." This was a direct reference to arguably Clausewitz's most famous dictum: "War is a mere continuation of policy by other means." In fact, a more accurate translation of the German word *Politik* is probably "politics" rather than "policy"; nor is this mere semantics. "Policy" conveys an impression of direction and clear intent; "politics," like war, is an adversarial business whose implementation, also like war, is often messy and confused.

In truth Clausewitz changes his mind about the effect of politics on war. In Book 1 of *On War* he states that it permeates war and moderates it. But Book 8, written later, contains the contradictory view that the politics of the French Revolution had made war more destructive, not less so. It also highlights the reciprocal nature of the relationship between war and politics: war should, in theory, be used as an instrument of politics; but once it breaks out and the political aims of each side clash, their reciprocity generates its own dynamic, feeding on hatred, on chance, and on the play of military probabilities. In other words war has its own nature, and can have very different consequences from the political aims that are meant to be guiding it.

Powell and Summers' misreading of Clausewitz was soon to have a very real (and ultimately detrimental) effect on US foreign policy. In 1983 Powell became the senior military assistant to the Secretary of Defense, Caspar Weinberger. Like Powell, Weinberger was determined to put the army back on its feet and found inspiration in *On War*. In late 1984 he laid down the following criteria for the use of American troops abroad: "As Clausewitz wrote, 'No one starts a war—or rather, no one in his senses ought to do so—without first being clear in his mind what he intends to achieve by that war, and how he intends to conduct it'." In Powell's opinion, the failure to do this was "mistake number one." It "led to Clausewitz's rule number two: Political leaders must set a war's objectives, while the armies achieve them."

Powell and Weinberger were attracted to Clausewitz because he seemed to be so clear about the relationship between war and politics. Yet their assumption that Clausewitz's "strange trinity" of war required a government as one of its elements made it hard for them to adjust to the reality of the post-Cold War period, from 1989 onwards, as wars were increasingly waged by non-state actors such as guerrillas, terrorists, and warlords. So when Bosnian Serb irregulars began to slaughter Muslims in the former Yugoslavia in 1992, and the American public called for military intervention, Colin Powell (by now Chairman of the US Joint Chiefs) repeated the Weinberger doctrine that clear political objectives were required before he was prepared to commit US ground troops, thereby costing countless innocent lives.

But Powell went further: he rejected the use of "limited force," stating instead that "decisive means and results are always to be preferred." This was the second of the US Army's intellectual responses to defeat in Vietnam: a rethinking of its operational doctrine that took as its model the pre-1945 German

Army. Powell and others were particularly taken with the Prussian (later German) General Staff's preoccupation with what it called a "strategy of annihilation," the achievement of a victory on the battlefield so decisive and so speedy it would determine the political outcome. This, too, was an idea traced back to Clausewitz. What it ignored, however, was Clausewitz's acceptance towards the end of his life (and an idea he pursues in Book 8 of *On War*), that the waging of a limited war (or even a war of observation, i.e. using the threat of war) was an equally valid means of achieving the same political end. Moreover at no stage does he suggest that soldiers should be left, unfettered by politicians, to fight war without political direction (or interference); on the contrary, Clausewitz argues that the commander-in-chief should be in the cabinet so that the politicians can share in decisions concerning strategy.

By 1992, two currents with a Clausewitzian pedigree had converged in the Powell doctrine: one embracing the political purpose of war and the other the way it should be fought. Yet by the dawn of the new millennium the US Army, increasingly conscious of its pre-eminence in the world, had begun to concentrate on the second current, "decisive means and results," to the detriment of the first. Thus, as

Hew Strachan has noted, the planning and implementation of the invasion of Iraq in 2003 revealed an almost willful pursuit of "rapid operational success" by General Tommy Franks, the US commander, at "the expense of long-term political goals" (not the least of which was the postwar political settlement, i.e. who and what would replace Saddam Hussein as Iraq's ruler). Franks later explained that "the maxims of the Prussian strategist Carl von Clausewitz had dictated that mass—concentrated formations of troops and guns—was the key to victory. To achieve victory, Clausewitz advised, a military power must mass its forces at the enemy's "center of gravity." But this was to ignore both the political dimension of war, and the fact that, as explained above, Clausewitz eventually realized there was more than one way for a combatant to use (or threaten to use) force.

By ignoring, or failing to understand, Clausewitz's central point that a general's main task was to use military operations to achieve his government's political aims, Franks fought the Iraq War of 2003 in a virtual political vacuum, treating the campaign almost as an end in itself. Seven years later in Afghanistan a similar scenario played itself out during the US troop "surge" when General David Petraeus was given the military means to deliver greater security, but not the coherent policy objectives that would enable him to "win" the war. Sherard Cowper-Coles, Britain's Ambassador to Afghanistan from 2007 to 2009, wrote later: "Just plunging on with a strategy of pouring in more troops and more money without doing something about governance and about the political offer to the Afghan people and [...] regional players, was a recipe for eventual failure."

What, then, of future warfare and how can an understanding of Clausewitzian "strategy" help us to avoid the mistakes of the past? By adhering, I would suggest, to the following rules:

Firstly, that the decision to go to war—or rather to use lethal force to impose our will on an opponent—should only be taken if the true (and uncertain) nature of conflict is understood (in particular its tendency to create a dynamic of its own that can result in policy and logic being entirely suppressed by passion and emotion), if all other options (particularly diplomatic) have been exhausted, and we have clear, carefully thought-out and attainable political objectives in view.

Secondly, that there is no ideal mode of warfare by which we might achieve these political objectives, and that, depending upon the circumstances, everything from wars of observation (such as the Cold War), through limited wars (such as the air operations in Libya), to total or absolute war (in which the whole of society is engaged, such as the two world wars) might be necessary.

Thirdly, that a military commander's strategy is devoted to linking tactics and operations (or the mode of fighting) to political objectives, or as Clausewitz put it: "The political view is the object, War, is the means, and the means must always include the object in our conception."

CHAPTER 8

STRATEGIES FOR UNCERTAIN TIMES THROUGH THE EXAMPLE OF THE FINANCIAL SYSTEM

JÖRG ROCHOLL

The manifest crisis in the Eurozone is now in its fourth year. In terms of the global financial crisis we are already entering the seventh year. The continuation of this financial crisis over such a long period of time, varying in form and intensity, illustrates the urgency of the question of how the possibility of failure can be included in the calculations of actors operating in politics and in the financial markets, and what strategies are needed for uncertain times.

THE POSSIBILITY OF FAILURE IS EXTREMELY RELEVANT

The timeliness of this subject is demonstrated by the present situation in the European financial markets. The extraordinary measures taken by the European Central Bank (ECB) have, of course, relieved the situation noticeably, but the current atmosphere of calm could quickly turn out to be deceptive. Thus reforms must be undertaken that in particular can remedy the errors committed when the Euro was set up, replacing the ad hoc measures that are all too frequently employed. Generally speaking, dealing with downturns is a primary task of the financial markets. The shareholders assign their capital hoping for returns and that their company will enjoy long-term success. Creditors and banks lend capital under exactly the same conditions. Even for rating agencies and analysts failure is always a central component in their deliberations. When assessing the interaction between risk (as a gauge of failure) and returns, the higher the risk, the higher the returns. To put it another way, if I want to persuade an investor to put money into a riskier type of investment, then I have to offer a higher return than would be the case with a less risky type of investment. In addition, the financial markets have drawn up a series of principles based on the experiences of everyday life. The central idea is that failure is as far as possible to be prevented. However, if it cannot be prevented, then the degree of damage should at least be limited. The following four principles are of relevance here:

Principle 1: The party that makes a return also bears the risk. The party that takes a risk also reaps the returns. The establishment of a company is always linked to the incentive of profiting from one's own work. The possibility of failure can thus be seen as the catalyst for a particularly high investment, as every entrepreneur knows that if it does not work he must start over again.

Principle 2: There is a strong incentive to diversify risk, following the saying: "Never put all your eggs in one basket."

Principle 3: Risk can only be compensated for when the holding is undiversifiable, in what is known as systematic risk. A classic example concerns a parasol manufacturer and an umbrella manufacturer. Share-holding investors in both these companies cannot expect compensation for bad or good weather, as they can eliminate the risk factor of the weather by investing in both companies. However, these invest-ments will not protect them against systematic risks such as an economic collapse. This principle is fundamental to the pricing of financial investments.

Principle 4: It is important to build in buffers. As Donald Rumsfeld said, there exist so-called "unknown unknowns." These are relevant precisely when considering banks' requests to increase their equity capital.

The basic premise of these principles, however, is the following: whoever makes a return must also bear the risk. The question is whether this relationship still applies today, or whether it is possible that failure is no longer such a great tragedy? In that case, as an investor, either I make a return or others underwrite my losses if my strategy should turn out to be a failure. Must I deal with failure at all? And if not, what does this mean for my investment strategy? Does this mean I can take on higher risks?

Primarily this is a question of the unification of ownership and liability, that is the basic market-economy principle that has been infringed since the Euro was introduced. Nowhere is this clearer than if we look at the yield spreads between the government bonds of the different Euro states. Indeed, if the principle of no bailout (as a kind of collective strategy), i.e. the prohibition of countries assuming liability for the obligations of another country, had really been valid, then yield spreads between the German and Greek government bonds, for example, would have had to have been considerably higher over a long period of time. Clearly this was not the case. The background is that the capital markets factored into their prices that in the case of one country being over-indebted, other countries will and must step in, as a payment default would have had a devastating impact on the lenders and thus on the stability of the financial market. Thus, despite being underpinned by a treaty, the no-bailout principle was never realistic. Equally apparent is the damage done to the unification of ownership and liability through the publishing of bank ratings. The overall rating actually consists of two elements: on the one hand the rating of a bank's inherent strengths and on the other the support available to these banks from their respective countries of origin in the case of failure.

In both cases risks are incurred at the expense of third parties, in this instance the taxpayer. This is accompanied by a transfer of risk from the private to the public sector; and pricing is distorted by this risk transfer. It is thus extremely important to find a way of reunifying ownership and liability. Here the particular challenge is to create clear rules that will be adhered to in the event of a crisis. We shall now look at this question in detail.

EXCESSIVE DEBT AT ALL LEVELS AS A FUNDAMENTAL PROBLEM

It is frequently said today that we have to combat the sovereign debt crisis. This is certainly correct, as in the end the sovereign debt ratios in Europe and the rest of the world are undoubtedly too high. Greece, with a debt ratio of 157% of gross domestic product (GDP) in the fourth quarter of 2012, is not the only example; in addition, apparently as if it were the most natural thing in the world, and even according to official figures, almost all other countries in the Eurozone are now well above the Maastricht criterion of 60% for government debt; Italy is on 127%; Ireland 118%; Portugal 124%, and even the supposed role model Germany is on 82%. The trend is upward.

Already the level of these quotas suggests that the debt did not come about overnight. Therefore this is not merely a consequence of the financial crisis. An historical assessment of Germany and other European countries also makes this clear. As recently as the 1970s the sovereign debt of many countries, including Germany, started to increase considerably. At the beginning of the 1970s the sovereign debt ratio in Germany was still below 20%. Up until German reunification it rose to around 40%, and since then has doubled once again. At this point we should deal immediately with both a rumor and a possible political argument: this development is not a consequence of the state's diminishing grasp on overall economic output, as between 1970 and 2010 output grew sevenfold. At the same time state revenues rose by a factor of seven and a half. Thus the state controls an even greater proportion of economic output, but nevertheless increases its debts, as state expenditure increased eightfold over this same period of time.

While it is certainly correct to combat the sovereign debt crisis, equally we should not forget that a one-sided approach to sovereign debt does not go far enough. Experts and rating agencies agree on how difficult it is to assign ratings to government bonds. Even after many decades of research, the forecast capability in this area is shockingly low, quite the opposite of assigning ratings in the case of corporate bonds where the degree of corporate indebtedness and the company's ability to pay interest from its corporate profits can account for 40% of a particular rating. The situation with regard to states is more complicated, as here questions of political and social stability play a major role. One point, however, is clear: to understand the development of a state's creditworthiness, it is extremely important to take a look at the condition of its private sector. Only an understanding of the extent to which the private sector is indebted and how strongly it can grow will produce a better understanding of how the state in question is performing.

To substantiate this insight, it is worth taking a look at Europe. Many of the countries that are suffering today as a result of particular challenges seemed like "grade A students" in the area of sovereign debt up until the start of the economic and financial crisis in 2007/08. For example, if we look at how frequently individual European countries failed to meet the Maastricht deficit criterion of a maximum new borrowing limit of 3% of GDP between the introduction of the Euro in 1999 and 2009, that is before the sovereign debt crisis became apparent, then we see something that is familiar but also surprising. Occupying first place in these statistics, unsurprisingly, is Greece, a country that failed to meet the deficit criterion nine times in the period in question. We might note in passing that it can be assumed that fulfillment of the deficit criterion in other years was only guaranteed on paper. In second place—again unsurprisingly—is Italy, with six infringements, closely followed by Germany, among others, with five infringements. Looking for Spain on this list, we have to go further down to see that Spain, during the period in question, failed to meet the deficit criterion only twice; and the same goes for Ireland. Both countries can claim with some justification that until the crisis hit they were to a certain extent "poster children" for the rest of Europe. Spain even ran a budget surplus between 2005 and 2007. This trend is reflected in the total government debt of these countries before 2008, as in each case these values were considerably less than that of Germany and below the Maastricht criterion of total government debt as 60% of GDP.

Thus it is clear that other factors are playing a major role here. In both countries the current sovereign debt ratios that are far higher than those of 2008 can only be explained through the large burdens that resulted, and still result, from the aid packages given to the domestic banking sector. Thus the sovereign debt crisis in these countries is not, as once generally thought, a short-term crisis in liquidity, but fundamentally a banking crisis. In these cases at least burdens in the banking sector must be regarded as a (limited) liability for state finances.

THE CLOSE RELATIONSHIP BETWEEN BANKS AND STATES AS A CATALYST

This problem is primarily a result of the close relationship between states and banks *and* the close relationships between the banks themselves.

NO DIVERSIFICATION: PART ONE

The problem of the close relationship between states and banks is first and foremost a product of the assets on the banks' balance sheets, as banks invest heavily—too heavily—in European government bonds. This can also be explained by reasons of regulation: first, for banks investing in government bonds there is no equity capital investment, at least in the majority of cases this is so. Second—and this is probably more serious—there is no restriction in the amount invested in government bonds. Even in Basel III, in Article 109/145 on Capital Requirement Regulation, these two fundamental rules have not been changed.

If we look at the situation in practice, we can see how quickly the absence of such restrictions makes itself felt. Looking at the results of the stress tests carried out by the European Banking Authority (EBA) in December 2011, we might ask how investments in government bonds relate to the banks' equity capital.

To answer this question let us look at the example of various countries. In the Greek banks that were included in the stress test, four times the amount of equity capital was invested in Greek government bonds. In Portugal the figure is more than three times; in Spain and Italy, for example, one and a half times; in Cyprus something more than four times. In Germany, however, only about half the amount of equity capital was invested in domestic government bonds; the rest presumably overwhelmingly in Greek bonds. To all appearances the ECB's massive injections of liquidity have only exacerbated this trend further, as banks frequently use this liquidity to buy up even more government bonds. It thus becomes clear that the problems of states and government bonds inevitably have an effect on the banking system of the respective country as well. Of course, the problems can also be fuelled by other reasons. We only have to look at the property market and the banks in Spain and Ireland and, equally, at the German Landesbanken; that is, at cases where banking problems have turned into national problems.

In light of the assets on the banks' balance sheets it is crucial that consideration be given to diversification, that is limiting investment in government bonds, and that banks are not given further incentives to buy up even more such securities. This is particularly applicable in the case of the conditions regarding the "liquidity coverage ratio," the question of in what form banks should maintain liquidity reserves in future. It is inconceivable that government bonds should play any kind of central role in this case.

Let us now turn to the liabilities on the banks' balance sheet and in particular to the banks' creditors. As we have already seen, problems can also be caused by the banks. The question is: what happens if the banks get into difficulties and must be restructured or liquidated? In this situation we must unfortunately admit that despite all attempts and despite the restructuring law—for example in Germany—real creditor participation is still an absolute exception. The OECD (Organisation for Economic Co-operation and Development) has produced a study on this subject.[1] It shows that creditor participation took place more than once (that is in more than one bank) in only four states—Denmark, Iceland, Great Britain, and the USA. That means that as a rule creditors are not involved in what happens to banks and the financial system when they get into difficulties—and if they do it is only to a very limited extent. If they do, creditors seem only to have been involved in the case of smaller banks thus far; in the case of larger banks they were overwhelmingly compensated by the state. This leads to a vicious circle: the banks who can no longer control the risks they have undertaken cause problems for their own countries by transferring their burdens onto the state. As a result the situation worsens for the states and this has an effect on government bonds, leading to problems for the banks who hold these bonds.

Let us look at the case of individual countries. In Ireland, for example, according to Achim Dübel's calculations, only around 10% of the capital requirements of Irish banks could be covered by a bail-in.[2] As such, this is an exception that currently has to be regarded as something positive. By contrast, the process in Spain has happened much more slowly. Here the participation of creditors has been shelved, perhaps because, unlike in Ireland, it was primarily domestic investors who were affected. In any case the result of this delay is that some of the investors could sell off their shares to retail investors, who in turn were protected politically. Italy, too, seems to have given no priority to a bail-in. In this context we need only think of the case of the Banca Monte dei Paschi di Siena. Here the estimated creditor losses amount to a fraction of the state's losses.

In the case of Cyprus, again the above situation applies. Even if the implementation of creditor participation is in principle to be welcomed, the problems are managed in an ad hoc fashion without clear rules, although such rules might be expected—also in the case of problems affecting other countries in the future. For example, participation was not implemented according to the seniority of internal and thereafter external equity providers. Ultimately, even an initially agreed (then rejected) investor participation to the tune of less than €100,000 did nothing to restore confidence.

There are two conclusions that emerge from these considerations. First, when banks get into difficulties creditor participation has so far largely failed to materialize. Second, the rescue and aid packages undertaken up to now have followed no clear rules. There is thus a pressing need for a consistent system of regulation at international level, such as the EU's Recovery and Resolution Directive (RRD). What is crucial in this case, however, is not only the adoption of such a system of regulation, but above all its implementation. Particularly in the case of the RRD the possibility of a bail-in is still not being implemented to the necessary extent. According to the current suggestion, implementation is not supposed to take place until 2018. In the end, however, as the reverse argument shows, as long as this bail-in is not the norm but is instead shelved, this will result in even more risks for taxpayers. Once again, this means that there is an increasing transfer of risk between the banks' creditors and states' creditors, and taxpayers incur too great a burden.

NO DIVERSIFICATION: PART TWO

As this discussion shows, substantial creditor participation has thus far been unforthcoming, so we should now ask why this is the case. Undoubtedly political reasons play a major role here. But, in addition, there is the close relationship between the banks. A relevant study in this context is by Hildebrandt, Rocholl, and Schulz, where *all* the securities in *all* German banks were investigated, and it was revealed that 80% of the portfolio value of German banks is accounted for by securities investments in other banks.[3] By contrast, government bonds play merely a minor role. To this extent, alongside the close interrelationship between banks and states, we can also see an extremely close relationship and system of networks between the banks themselves, and thus a high degree of interdependence. This close relationship between banks can be seen as a fundamental challenge, and makes actual creditor participation in the case of banks particularly difficult, as the danger arises that this places a burden on those banks that are of systemic importance.

The recommendations of the Liikanen Report are thus to be warmly welcomed, as they concern the creation of a bail-in instrument that cannot be held by other banks.[4] Notwithstanding this recommendation, in Europe there are political reasons for putting the brakes on creditor participation—as in Spain. Such reasons encourage countries to wait and hope that the debt burden will at some point be taken up at European level.

CONCLUSION

The fundamental challenge in the Eurozone is to unify ownership and liability and thus protect the taxpayer. This goal has not yet been reached. Creditor participation, particularly in the case of bank insolvencies, has remained the exception, as this often created the fear that it would lead to other banks being affected. However, what is entailed is a transfer of risk from the private to the public sector that overburdens many states and creates a vicious circle that, in turn, has an effect on the solvency of the banks. Breaking down the close relationship between states and banks, and in particular the close interrelationship between the banks themselves, remains a major challenge on the road to a sustainably functioning Eurozone. Four goals above all should be met: the implementation of credible regulations rather than the application of ad hoc measures; strengthening of diversification within the banks; the creation of a large buffer zone by means of more equity capital; and the abolition of explicit and implicit state guarantees. The possibility of failure must be *real*, as this creates the strongest incentives for individuals to make decisions assuming full responsibility. In this way a further transfer of risk from the private to the public sector can be prevented.

Notes

1. Sebastian Schich and Kim Byoung-Hwan, "Developments in the Value of Implicit Guarantees for Bank Debt: The Role of Resolution Regimes and Practices," in *OECD Financial Market Trends*, issue 2, 2012.

2. Achim Dübel, "After the 'Whatever-it-takes' Bail-out of Eurozone Bank Bondholders," working paper, 2013.

3. Thomas Hildebrand, Jörg Rocholl, and Alexander Schulz, "Flight to Where? Evidence from Bank Investments during the Financial Crisis", working paper, 2012.

4. High-level Expert Group on Reforming the Structure of the EU Banking Sector, chaired by Erkki Liikanen, 2 October 2012.

CHAPTER 9

DANGEROUS WAGERS

KAI A. KONRAD

How do decision-makers react when faced with the threat of failure? What can a company do if its core business disintegrates? A decision simply to "carry on as before" will merely eat up the company's capital, and cost-cutting measures can only slow the process down. What can a speculator or bond dealer do when he has already built up huge losses in his positions? What can a bank do when it is sitting on a large portfolio of bad mortgage debts, or when it does not have a profitable business model? What can a political party or a government do when the electorate runs away because of the policies they have embarked upon? In all these very different contexts the problem of decision-making is very similar. Necessity is the mother of invention, as the saying goes. This maxim refers to a behavioral model that is common to all these situations.

Companies that have lost their business model like to look around for new areas of business. For many years German energy providers such as E.on and RWE, for example, had at least two stable main sources of income: nuclear energy and natural gas. With the turnaround in energy policy, nuclear power in Germany began to be phased out. In addition, with new technologies in oil and natural gas production the price structure of natural gas on the world markets changed enormously. Long-term supply contracts for natural gas suddenly became a burden.[1] In such situations companies have to reinvent themselves. It has been reported that E.on is looking abroad for new areas of business, such as in Brazil and other emerging countries.[2] Even if outsiders at least do not fully understand what constitutes the competitive advantage a company has in these new areas of business compared to local enterprises, the strategy makes sense from the company's point of view: without such ventures there is a real threat of failure.

A bank that is sitting on a large amount of bad debt can, of course, disclose the situation and admit defeat. However, it could be more interesting for the management to undertake a risky strategy that promises great success with a certain degree of probability, but that otherwise would cause serious losses. The financial markets offer many such possibilities. Such a business model offers a rescue opportunity. And if that does not work, one can do no more than fail. As a result of the collapse of Lehman Brothers, Hypo Real Estate in Germany learned how quickly success can turn into failure.[3]

It is not only companies that are familiar with this phenomenon and that succumb to its enticements. Over the past few years within the banks there have been several prominent examples of individual traders speculating in such a way that only a dangerous wager could bail them out. We do not know how often such bets have been placed; but we know about it when they fail. The venerable Barings Bank, for example, was badly hit by the speculative activities of Nick Leeson, a Singapore-based trader. According to reports, at the start he was able to hide his losses, but by the end, when the losses could no longer be concealed, they had grown to £1.3 billion.[4] The trader Jérôme Kerviel, who is reported to have lost as much as €5 billion at Société Générale, seems to present a similar case."[5]

We know of similar problems in the realm of politics as well. In light of a failing state economy that lasted almost twenty years, and a debt ratio of around 240% of economic output,[6] Japan embarked upon a macro-economic experiment that attracted a great deal of attention.

Under the title of "Abenomics" the government and the Japanese central bank began a concerted action. The central bank bought up quite considerable amounts of Japanese sovereign debt and the government put together a large debt-financed recovery plan. Many observers call this economic policy a "big bet."[7] The government hopes that in this way Japan can free itself from decades of ongoing economic failure through a Keynesian economic recovery and at the same time control its onerous debt burden. Many observers expect that this plan will not work out. Abenomics could quickly lead to the national bankruptcy of Japan.

The policy of saving the Euro, which Germany has been heavily involved in shaping, can also be seen as a desperate rescue attempt. The implementation of the no-bailout clause in light of Greece's threatening insolvency in spring 2010 could have probably led to the bankruptcy of several states within the Euro-zone. It would not have been pleasant for Germany either. By means of agreed steps towards the communitization of debt and the attempt to create European monitoring and control mechanisms in the area of state finances, it has been possible to avoid such events up until now. However, the long-term success of such measures is dubious. If the rescue attempt does not succeed, Germany will have to face the even higher costs of collapse.

Political economics is very familiar with such arguments, and has analyzed similar problems at a more general level. Politicians who have no luck with their domestic policies and who are threatened with failure can concentrate their activities in other areas. In an extreme case, as Hess and Orphanides (1995) point out,[8] a president can even take his country into an international conflict or war in order to avoid the threatened loss of power once again. Undoubtedly, some of the most dangerous and costly bets have involved taking enormous political risks in order to maintain one's position of power.

This long list of examples from very diverse areas reveals how decision-makers react to the threat of failure. The economic calculation behind all these decisions follows a uniform pattern that is sometimes described as "gambling for resurrection." This calculation is among the favorite strategies used in the face of failure, but it is also one of the most dangerous. Someone with their back against the wall can either give up and head for the safety of defeat, or enter into a bet. The bet promises rescue with a certain degree of probability. But there is also a residual probability of a huge amount of damage. One would not take on this bet if one did not need to, as the expected gain in the event of success is considerably smaller than the expected loss in the event of failure. The bet is actually a bet on financial loss. But for someone whose back is against the wall, this bet is attractive. He will profit if the bet succeeds; and he does not bear the loss himself if the bet is lost. Others will bear the loss, or at least the best part of it.

This calculation is dangerous as the decision-maker does not bear the costs that are incurred if the bet is lost; but the costs themselves do not simply vanish into thin air. They are assumed by other actors. In the case of banks that frequently means the taxpayers; in the case of companies it is usually the shareholders, lenders, and employees. In the case of bank traders it is the banks' shareholders so long as their financial backing lasts. In the case of private investors it is usually their business partners. In the case of bets placed by politicians and governments, in general it is the citizens and taxpayers who take responsibility for these dangerous wagers.

How should we deal with this phenomenon? We can tackle it on two levels. On the one hand we can demand more guarantees and assurances from the decision-makers. Those who have sufficient financial security must themselves bear most of the consequences of the negative outcome of a bet. This gives rise to a "margin of safety" away from the zone in which one agrees to "gamble for resurrection." The recommendation of Admati and Hellwig (2012) that the banks be provided with considerably more equity capital, for example, is completely in line with such a solution. More capital ensures that the losses resulting from the unfavorable outcome of a bet are borne by the owners of the banks themselves. This makes "bets on financial loss" less attractive from the point of view of the shareholders.[9]

Such "collateral solutions" will not always be possible. Dangerous wagers will, of course, become attractive when this security capital is used up. In addition, ownership structures and guarantees are often complex and many actors must inevitably make decisions whose financial and economic consequences exceed their own financial means enormously. This is particularly relevant in the realm of politics. No head of state has at his disposal financial reserves that he might use to cushion his country from the consequences of his political decisions. Thus the call for criminal responsibility often comes across loud and clear.

But even the threat of sanctions cannot really solve the problem. German insolvency law can use the offence of delayed insolvency to solve the problem. Anyone who delays the insolvency of a company can be punished. This can help as a deterrence. But for someone who nevertheless engages in delayed insolvency, gambling for resurrection only becomes even more attractive. Steep penalties might create a deterrence effect. But steep penalties threatening someone who is already in the middle of gambling for resurrection and fails present precisely the wrong kind of incentive for such people. They encourage flights of the imagination in situations when one is considering taking on an even bigger "gamble for resurrection."

Thus the solution must be to take away the instrument of "gambling for resurrection" from decision-makers who are close to going under. Transparency and early powers of intervention could help. If a threatened bankruptcy becomes transparent early on one can perhaps intervene and take the possibility of an expensive "gamble for resurrection" away from the decision-maker.

At the level of politics the problem is more difficult. Here there are unfortunately only a few possible ways of preventing the policy of gambling for resurrection. A central question remains of how, in these areas, we can increase the extent of personal responsibility and create intervention mechanisms in order to prevent actors entering into dangerous wagers.

Notes

1. The German energy provider RWE, for example, managed to withdraw from and renegotiate these contracts via an international court of arbitration. See "RWE und Gazprom rufen Schiedsgericht an," in *manager magazin online*, 7 June 2013, http://www.manager-magazin.de/unternehmen/energie/a-904354.html and "RWE bekommt Milliarden-Rückzahlung von Gazprom," in *Spiegel-Online*, 18 September 2013, 17:52, http://www.spiegel.de/wirtschaft/unternehmen/rwe-bekommt-milliarden-rueckzahlung-von-gazprom-a-923072.html

2. "E.on drängt nach Brasilien," in *Spiegel-Online*, 11 January 2012, 17.35, http://www.spiegel.de/wirtschaft/unternehmen/neue-strategie-e-on-drängt-nach-brasilien-a-808594.html

3. Cf., for example, "Riskante Wetten bringen Hypo Real Estate ins Wanken," in *Handelsblatt online*, 29 September

2008, 17:24, http://www.handelsblatt.com/unternehmen/banken/hintergrund-riskante-wetten-bringen-hypo-real-estate-ins-wanken/3028596.html
"Warum der Geldmarkt der HRE zu schaffen macht," in *Spiegel-Online*, 5 October 2008, 09:47, http://www.spiegel.de/wirtschaft/hintergrund-warum-der-geldmarkt-der-hre-zu-schaffen-macht-a-582246.html

4. "Kleiner Händler verzockt ganz großes Geld," in *Handelsblatt online*, 24 January 2008, 17:57, http://www.handelsblatt.com/unternehmen/banken/auf-den-spuren-von-nick-leeson-kleiner-haendler-verzockt-ganz-grosses-gelt/2891024.html
Katharina Wetzel, "Bankrott der Barings Bank, Über die peinlichste Zeit von Nick Leeson," in *Süddeutsche.de Wirtschaft*, 9 April 2013, 18:03, http://www.sueddeutsche.de/wirtschaft/2.220/bankrott-der-barings-bank-ueber-die-peinlichste-zeit-von-nick-leeson-1.1644825
Bettina Schulz, "Finanzskandale (7): Nick Leeson, 'Als handele man mit Seifenblasen'," in *faz-net*, 7 March 2009, http://www.faz.net/aktuell/finanzen/finanzskandale/finanzskandale-7-nick-leeson-als-handele-man-mit-seifenblasen-1149410.html

5. Polizei verhört Jérome Kerviel," in *manager magazin online*, 26 January 2008, http://www.manager-magazin.de/unternehmen/artikel/a-531192.html

6. Carsten Germis, "Japans Spiel mit dem Feuer," in *faz-net*, 1 March 2013, http://www.faz.net/aktuell/wirtschaft/wirtschaftspolitik/abenomics-japans-spiel-mit-dem-feuer-12098066.html

7. "Geldpolitik: Japans grosse Schuldenwette," in *zeit.de*, 22 January 2013, 11:26,

http://www.zeit.de/wirtschaft/2013-01/japan-geldpolitik-schulden

8. Gregory D. Hess and Athanasios Orphanides, "War Politics: an Economic, Rational-voter Framework," in *American Economic Review*, 85(4), (1995), pp. 828–46.

9. Anat Admati and Martin Hellwig, *The Bankers' New Clothes: What's Wrong with Banking and What to Do About It* (Princeton: Princeton University Press, 2013).

CHAPTER 10

SIMPLE SOLUTIONS FOR COMPLEX
PROBLEMS

GERD GIGERENZER

The search for certainty is an ancient human endeavor. It has produced magic rituals, fortune-tellers, and authority figures who know what is right and wrong. Similarly, for centuries many philosophers have gone astray as they searched for certainties where there are none or, as the distinguished proponent of philosophical pragmatism John Dewey demonstrated, equated knowledge with certainty and belief with uncertainty.

The problem is that false certainty can cause a great deal of damage. As we shall see, blind belief in tests and financial forecasts can, under certain circumstances, lead to a life of poverty and misery. Not only can it ruin our physical and mental health, but it can also ruin our bank account and the economy as a whole. We must learn to live with uncertainty and it is time we faced up to it. A first step is to clarify the difference between known and unknown risks.

The twilight of uncertainty contains a variety of different nuances and gradations. Since the 17th century the probabilistic revolution provided people with methods of statistical thinking that enabled them to triumph over fate. But these methods were designed only for the palest shades of uncertainty, for a world of *known risks*, or, simply, of *risks*. I am using this concept to describe a world where all alternatives, consequences, and probabilities are known. This is the case, for example, with lotteries and games of chance. However, most of the time we live in a changing world where some of these factors are unknown, so we have to deal with unknown risks or *uncertainty*.

By comparison with the world of risk, the world of uncertainty is enormous. Whom should we marry? Whom should we trust? What shall we do with the rest of our lives? In an uncertain world it is impossible to determine what the optimal course of action should be by means of an exact calculation of the risks. We have to deal with "unknown unknowns." Surprises are inevitable. But even when calculations provide no clear answers, we have to make decisions.

Alongside mathematical probability there is a second concept that is often overlooked: the rule of thumb or, in scientific terms, heuristics. Making good decisions requires two types of mental tools:

RISK: if the risks are known, good decisions need logical and statistical thinking.

UNCERTAINTY: if some risks are unknown, good decisions also require intuition and clever rules of thumb.

In most cases a combination of the two is needed. Some things can be calculated, others cannot, and what can be calculated is often only a rough estimate. In an uncertain world statistical thinking and the communication of risk is not enough. Good rules of thumb are vitally important for good decisions. A rule of thumb or *heuristic* allows us to make a decision quickly without much searching for information but nevertheless with a high degree of accuracy. This is completely different from a balance sheet approach that lists the pros and cons: it tries to single out the most important pieces of information and disregards the rest.

Every rule of thumb I know of can be used consciously and unconsciously. If it is used unconsciously, we talk about intuitive judgments. An intuition or a gut feeling is a judgment

1. That appears directly in our consciousness
2. That has underlying reasons we are not fully aware of
3. That is strong enough to act upon.

A gut feeling is neither a whim, nor a sixth sense, nor clairvoyance, nor the voice of God. It is a kind of unconscious intelligence. The assumption that intelligence is necessarily conscious and considered is a huge mistake.

In my opinion the basic principle of intuition consists of two elements:

1. Simple rules of thumb that take advantage of
2. The brain's evolved abilities.

This means that the mind can discover simple solutions for complex problems. Here intuition exploits an evolved ability of the brain called recognition memory. Experts often search for less information than novices do, and confine themselves to heuristics.

What is important here is that ignoring information can lead to better, quicker, and more reliable decisions.

One would think that research into intelligent heuristics would be a central part of many disciplines—but not at all. Curiously, most theories of rational decision-making, from economics to philosophy, look for answers by asking questions that only refer to known risks. In the social sciences a lot of thought is devoted to complicated logical and statistical systems, but almost none to heuristic thinking, and if it does happen then it is above all to show that heuristics are a cause of human errors and catastrophes.

After the probabilistic revolution we need a second revolution that will take heuristics seriously and that will finally equip people with the skills they need to deal with the entire range of uncertainties.

I call this next step the "heuristic revolution." In this we must learn to act in uncertain worlds using intelligent rules of thumb.

In order to make good decisions in an uncertain world we must disregard some of the information, and this is precisely what happens when we use rules of thumb. This saves time and effort *and* leads to better decision-making.

To summarize:

RULES OF THUMB ARE NOT STUPID. In an uncertain world simple rules of thumb can lead to better results than sophisticated calculations.

LESS IS MORE. Complex problems no longer need complex solutions. Look for simple solutions first of all.

I believe in the effectiveness of simple rules in a real, unmanageable world. Even if sometimes they do not always help, the first question should be: can we find a simple solution for a complex problem? We rarely ask this question. Our first reflex is to look for complex solutions, and when they do not work we make them even more complicated. The same applies in the world of investments. After turbulent times on the finance markets that not even experts were able to predict, simple rules of thumb offer an alternative. Let us look at a complex problem that many of us face. You have a certain amount of money you want to invest. You do not want to put it all on one horse, and are considering buying some shares. You want to diversify, but how?

Harry Markowitz was awarded the Nobel Prize in Economics for his work solving this problem. The solution is called a *mean-variance portfolio*. The portfolio maximizes the return (mean) and minimizes the risk (variance). In short the model tells you how you can expect to gain the highest return for the lowest risk. Many banks rely on this and similar investment methods, and warn their customers against trusting their intuition.

You might think that Markowitz, when he set up his own investments for his social security, would have used his Nobel Prize-winning method. But, no, he stuck to the simple rule of thumb of "1/N" which means you *allocate your money equally to each of N funds.*

Why did he rely on a heuristic rather than on calculations? In an interview Markowitz explained that he wanted to avoid blaming himself: "I thought, if stocks go up and I'm not in, I'll think I'm stupid. And if they fall and I'm not in, I'll think I'm stupid. So I decided to invest 50/50." He followed the motto of many investors: make it simple! And 1/N is not only simple, it is also the purest form of diversification.

How good is this rule of thumb? In a study it was compared with the mean-variance portfolio and a dozen other complex methods. Seven investment problems, such as investments in ten US industrial funds, were analyzed. In the mean-variance portfolio the stock data from the last ten years was consulted, while 1/N needs no data. And the result? In most of the seven tests 1/N scored better according to the usual performance criteria than the mean-variance method. Moreover, none of the other twelve complex methods consistently predicted the future value of the stocks more accurately.

So is the Nobel Prize-winning method a con? No. It works best in an ideal world of known risks, but not necessarily in the uncertain world of the stock market where so much is unknown. In this case the parameters of the portfolio must be extrapolated from earlier data. However, as we have seen, ten years is too short a period to produce reliable estimates. Let us suppose you invest in fifty funds. How many years of financial data would the mean-variance method need to perform better than 1/N? A computer simulation provides the answer: around 500 years! That means that in the year 2500 investors can progress from the simple rule to the higher math of the mean-variance model and thus hope to make a profit. But this only works if the same stocks—and the stock market—still exist.

The moral of the story is that in a world of known risks that corresponds to the mathematical assumptions of the mean-variance portfolio, it is worth doing the calculation. However, in the real of world of investments, simple intuitive rules can be smarter.

The same generally applies in uncertain worlds. How can a simple rule of thumb beat a Nobel Prize-winning method? Was that simple coincidence? No. There's a mathematical theory that tells us why and when simple is better. This is called the *bias-variance dilemma*. The essence of this theory is expressed in a quote that is attributed to Albert Einstein:

Everything should be made as simple as possible, but not simpler.

How far we should go in simplifying things depends on three attributes. First, the greater the uncertainty, the more we should simplify. The lower the uncertainty, the more complex the method should be. Second, the more alternatives there are, the more we should simplify; if there are fewer alternatives, it is possible to be more complex. This is because complex methods have to estimate risk factors, and a greater number of alternatives means that more factors must be estimated, which leads to more errors in estimation.

High uncertainty	Low uncertainty
Many alternatives	Few alternatives
Small amount of data	Large amount of data
Make it simple	**Make it complex**

All this helps us to understand a general rule—the bias-variance problem, as the statisticians call it. When we use a particular method to make a prediction, we call the difference between the prediction and the actual outcome (which we could not know in advance) "bias."

In an uncertain world, bias is inevitable (in which case a happy accident helps). But there is also another kind of error, which we call "variance." Unlike 1/N, complex methods predict the future by means of previous observations. The prognoses depend on the specific sample of already established observations, and thus can be unstable. This instability (the variability of its mean value) is a called variance. Thus the more complex the method, the more factors must be estimated and the higher the number of variance errors becomes. 1/N always delivers the same stable recommendation, as the method needs no past investment data. For this reason it is not compromised by variance. If the quantity of data is very big—for example covering 500 years—instability is reduced to the extent that the complexity eventually pays off. Einstein's rule is a general formulation of the fact that, in an uncertain world, less can be more.

Taking intuition seriously means accepting the fact that it is a form of intelligence that one cannot articulate. If someone having good and long experience also has a bad gut feeling, don't ask why.

In my own research I have come to the following conclusion:

1. Intuition is neither a whim nor the source of every bad decision. It is unconscious intelligence that makes use of most parts of our brain.
2. Intuition is not inferior to logical thinking. In most cases both are necessary. Intuition is inevitable in a complex, uncertain world, while logic can be sufficient in a world in which all risks are known with certainty.
3. Intuition is not based on faulty mental software, but on intelligent rules of thumb and a lot of experience that lies hidden in our unconscious.

NOTE

This text is based on the book by Gerd Gigerenzer, *Risiko: Wie man die richtigen Entscheidungen trifft* © 2013 C. Bertelsmann Verlag, München, in the publishing group Random House GmbH.

CHAPTER 11

STRATEGIC MANAGEMENT IN THE FACE OF UNCERTAINTY

BURKHARD SCHWENKER

The challenge of managing companies has grown considerably tougher in recent years as complexity has increased on all sides. That is not to say managing was ever easy. We have always had to deal with upheavals and transitions: the Renaissance, the Industrial Revolution, the student protest movement in the late 1960s and the oil price shock in the 1970s, are just a few examples. Nor was communication "at your fingertips" in those days, which gave rise to information asymmetries that no longer exist today.

Today we face a phenomenon that really makes life (or planning, management) hard for us: uncertainty. Uncertainty means that we neither know what might happen, nor how probable it is that something might happen. Uncertainty thus goes far beyond mere *risk* and *unpredictability*—both terms we are more than familiar with. We talk about *risk* when a number of events are possible but when we know the probability that they will occur. Normal (or Gaussian) distribution is the measure of such calculable risks. And since we know the various possibilities, we can work out which decision is the better one. In the case of *unpredictability*, a number of events are once again possible. Unlike with *risk*, however, it is either difficult or impossible to calculate the probability that they will occur. Extrapolation is therefore possible only to a limited extent, and cause and effect relationships often only come to light after the event. But at least we have some idea of what might lie ahead.

And it's this difference between uncertainty and unpredictability that drives complexity. In the case of uncertainty, we don't know how likely it is that events will happen, but we also don't even know what those events might be. At this level of complexity, developments unfold in a non-linear fashion. It is impossible to predict either the direction or speed of events, which means that quantitative models and calculations alone will no longer help us. We need to look elsewhere. John Maynard Keynes wrote that "comparisons of quantity fail us, small changes produce large effects, the assumptions of a uniform and homogeneous continuum are not satisfied."

We see this every day in the practice of corporate management. Let me give you just a couple of examples: Ten years ago, who would have thought that the Internet would revolutionize retail and the media after all—alongside so many other industries—or that it would do so at such a frantic pace? Who would have thought that green technology would shape our growth trajectory, or that Germany would, once and for all, pull the plug on nuclear energy?

Who would have thought that China would become the world's leading exporter and that America would herald the advent of the Pacific Age? Or that shale gas and fracking would turn international energy markets on their head—causing American industry to sharpen its competitive edge so fast that many growth forecasts and competitive strategies, too, now have to be rethought?

There is almost no end to the list of unexpected developments, and of forecasts that are rendered obsolete at ever greater speed. These examples reflect the contradictions with which managers must these days come to terms. The issue, as I see it, is this: as managers we know that the future is uncertain. Yet precisely because this is so, the people in our companies feel a need for security that we must address. We know from painful experience that trends and numbers can no longer be relied on. Yet we still have to plan, make calculations and decide about investments. We know that an interdisciplinary mindset is the only way to stay abreast of the complex world in which we live. Yet at the same time, in-depth expertise and practical experience—functional skills, in other words—are necessary if we are to properly steer our companies' day-to-day business.

In my opinion, this circle can be squared with a piece of good news: corporate management is once again becoming more direct, more personal, more entrepreneurial. It can no longer hide behind models, concepts, "techniques" or even consultants. On the contrary, it demands personality, courage, and the ability to think and reflect. Managers must nail their colors to the mast. They need to have convictions. That is what I see as one of the best ways to deal with uncertainty.

If what I am saying is true, we must call into question the strategic and planning concepts we hold so dear. If uncertainty is what lies ahead, it makes little sense to calculate detailed figures for a strategic ten-year plan, or to base investment decisions primarily on quantitative calculations. No, we need to find new approaches, think in new directions—not that there is any lack of concepts or "strategic orientations": until the early 1990s, diversification was the credo that shaped strategic corporate thinking. It was followed by a concentration on "core competencies," combined with every conceivable variation on the theme of re-engineering and/or corporate transformation. The heady days of the New Economy then triggered the "deconstruction" of the value chain, later giving way to a renewed concentration on core business. Who knows, perhaps diversification, too, is now back on the menu. And while we also saw a trend toward corporate decentralization for a time, centralization now seems to be regaining the upper hand.

This constant stream of alternative strategy concepts leads many to conclude that corporate management is subject to fashion fads masterminded, by no means least, by consulting firms. I may not be objective on this point, but I do not believe this is so. Why? Because (almost) every one of the listed concepts had its rightful place at the time and given the prevailing conditions. Today, the problem is, rather, that such stable conditions no longer exist. This being the case, strategy development also involves recognizing when a concept no longer fits —and having the courage to go against the flow of both public opinion and analysts' views and switching to a new concept. Or switching to an old one that might be just the right thing for the current situation.

The same goes for the shareholder value concepts that were missing from my list. Which is why great credit is due to Jack Welch, former CEO of General Electric and perhaps the best-known proponent of the American-born shareholder value philosophy, for making the following admission in the darkest days of the financial crisis: "On the face of it, shareholder value is the dumbest idea in the world. Shareholder value is a result, not a strategy (…). The main pillars are your employees, your customers and your products."

Yet as true as it may be that a company's success depends on motivated people, excited customers and superior products, we still have to achieve these goals and be able to plot the right strategy. If we can no longer rely on trends, then numbers as planning assumptions and decision input will be of only limited use. What use is the analytical elegance of capital market models if the time series for future cashflows are increasingly unpredictable? If numbers cannot help us, we must acquire a feel for technologies, for what customers need and for underlying economic and sociopolitical developments. Albert Einstein's famous saying is more valid today than ever before: "Not everything that can be counted counts, and not everything that counts can be counted." Ultimately, if the people in our companies are unsettled by uncertainty, trust in the capabilities of management in particular plays a pivotal role.

The last point is particularly important to me, because I believe every one of us has a longing for security: for a secure income, solid career prospects, a future we can visualize and look forward to. In the past, it was easier to respond to this need for security. We could stand up in front of our team and make clear statements: "This is our strategy, these are the figures we want to achieve, and this is what we intend to do to accomplish our goal." And because the prevailing conditions were (more) stable, we even had a chance of keeping what we had promised. In other words, we were able to reduce complexity and communicate a sense of security.

I see org charts as a symbol of how we strive for security—and of the contradictions that are inherent in this striving today. We have known for years that we must be process-oriented in the way we run our companies, assigning tasks flexibly and avoiding structures that are set in stone. Yet virtually every company still has an organization chart, with all its neat little boxes and lines and names. Why? Because an org chart speaks of security. Look, that's my little box, my name. That's my home. That's where I belong.

The problem today is that we can no longer say whether such an org chart has any lasting value, any more than the supposedly reliable planning figures that used to let us reduce complexity. So we need something new to give us security. And to my mind, this something can only be the personality of leaders and managers themselves. These days, no one can hide behind a number or a plan. All managers must be able to explain their convictions and how they see the future, and, to do so, they need both a broad horizon and the courage to make it known. That in itself is not always easy. As Joseph Schumpeter once fittingly said: "Those who talk about their visions reveal the limits of their horizon." They must also be able to communicate a sense of security and nurture trust by making it clear that they are willing to deal with complex situations—and by showing that they have the integrity to tackle these situations in the best interests of the company and its people.

In an age of uncertainty, strategy development thus poses a dilemma: our strategies must be robust enough to create an adequate structure and foster trust. On the other hand, they must initially avoid or delay binding commitments to help the company stay as adaptable as possible. The core question is therefore: how do we create stability without sacrificing agility?

I believe three things are needed.

First, we need a strategic core that defines a company's key capabilities and positioning. This provides orientation both within the company and to the outside world. Take the example of Bosch: the company's three strategic cornerstones are a strong international presence, diversification focused on its technological core competencies, and powerful innovation capabilities. All three cornerstones have been built to last—they speak of longevity and sustainability. Thus it was that, when other companies "started flying by the seat of their pants" during the 2008–9 crisis, Franz Fehrenbach, then CEO, held fast to the company's fundamental principles: important research and development projects were continued and the strategic core remained intact.

Alongside a strategic core, a company also needs a measure of elasticity that lets it adapt to a changing environment without threatening this clearly defined core. Organizational theorists speak of "organizational slack," which they see as a very positive thing. They are referring to a surplus of resources—human and capital resources and skills—that are not strictly needed for the day-to-day business, and that are therefore free to address interdisciplinary topics or tackle innovative solutions to pressing problems.

Having said that, the meaning of the term "organizational slack" shifted when it came to Europe and to Germany. "Slack" has a negative connotation. It is antithetical to efficiency and must be eliminated. But we have overdone the efficiency side and sometimes oversimplified the issues involved. What do I mean? It is precisely this organizational slack that makes a company resilient by giving it the strategic reserves it needs to weather crises, or to build up completely new areas of competency when the pressure to change becomes irresistible. Don't get me wrong! I am not advocating a lackadaisical, hands-off approach. I am throwing out a challenge: the challenge of finding out how much slack should be accepted and precisely where. Properly managed, the resultant redundancy and freedom can help create new capabilities and fuel innovation—helping a company to cope with an uncertain world as a result.

A strategic core and strategic reserves are thus important to give a company a healthy balance between stability and agility. For me, though, the real answer to uncertainty and the resultant complexity is good management, even if that does not sound particularly innovative. After all, recognizing and mastering change is unquestionably the most important, the most essential task of top management. Yet it is precisely here that we find the main reasons why companies and strategies fail. Early warning signals pointing to changes in markets or technologies are overlooked or even actively suppressed. Regulatory and/or political influences on future corporate development are systematically underestimated. Changes in the customer and market landscape do not receive (adequate) boardroom attention. Managers respond too tentatively even to noticeable changes, tending to act hastily for the sake of doing something and putting on a show rather than taking considered and appropriate action.

None of these reasons come as a surprise, nor are the lessons we can learn from them anything new. It is not change as such that leads to failure, but the inability to recognize change in good time and respond resolutely and courageously. I am reminded of Barbara Tuchman's remarkable analytical work

The March of Folly, in which she concludes that gross strategic errors—from Troy to Vietnam—are attributable not to a lack of knowledge, nor to the absence of information signals, but to decision-makers who fall at the hurdle of either their own ego and/or the institutional conditions that surround them.

The conclusion I draw is that new strategic impulses, new tools, and new processes are less important than managers who have the courage to stand up for what they believe in, who do not hide behind methods and concepts (or even consultants, on occasion). Managers whose behavior and values instill a sense of security in the people they lead. Managers who have not forgotten the art of critical reflection and who can thus assess the reliability of strategic tools.

When the issue is dealing with uncertainty, good management is management that is less technocratic, more accessible to people and closer to the business, the clients and the technologies used. It is more personal, more direct, and more entrepreneurial. Being entrepreneurial alone is not enough, however. If we want to take a resolute stand in the face of uncertainty, we must combine this spirit with emotional sensitivity and stability, lucid self-reflection and, above all, openness to other life contexts and cultures. In other words, we need a more inter-disciplinary approach. We need a superior blend of business management, economic, geopolitical, and sociopolitical concepts.

Building bridges between all these disciplines is a huge challenge. Careful reflection and interdiscipli-nary thinking don't just materialize out of thin air. We must point our day-to-day work in this direction, and we must do the same with the training and devel-opment we give to our managers. Our universities must dare to return to more theory, laying philosoph-ical foundations and placing emphasis on analytical models of thought. At the same time, we must realign our companies' recruiting policies. The focus should no longer (only) be on "picture-perfect résumés," short periods of study, practical knowledge, and suit-able internships. It should also deliberately include the rough edges and sharp corners that come with experience of different disciplines and other walks of life. What use is "practical" training based solely on case studies? It is intrinsically backward looking, whereas the world around us moves relentlessly forward and is changing ever faster. And what do you do when forecasts are no longer valid, or inherited explanations no longer answer today's questions? We have to form our own opinion. The catch is that we can only do so if we have first learned to look beyond our own backyard and see how things interrelate.

Finally, dealing with uncertainty needs one more ingredient: optimism! Why optimism? Because uncertainty is first and foremost an opportunity. It opens up new and hitherto unknown possibilities—provided we have the courage and, above all, the conviction to embrace them!

CONTRIBUTORS

Prof. Dr. Jens Beckert has been Director of the Max Planck Institute for the Study of Societies in Cologne since 2005. He studied sociology and business studies in Berlin, New York, and Princeton. He gained his doctorate in 1996 and his postdoctoral qualification in sociology at the Free University, Berlin, in 2003. Before his appointment to the Max Planck Institute he held professorships in both Bremen and Göttingen. He has held research fellowships at prestigious American and European universities, including Harvard and Sciences Po in Paris. His research interests concern the areas of economic sociology and the sociology of inheritance. His numerous publications include *Erben in der Leistungsgesellschaft* (2013), and many essays on economic sociology and the sociology of markets, for example "Wirtschaftssoziologie als Gesellschaftstheorie" (2009, in *Zeitschrift für Soziologie*) and "The Social Order of Markets" (2009, in *Theory and Society*).

Prof. Dr. Bazon Brock is Emeritus Professor of Aesthetics and Cultural Education at the Bergische Universität in Wuppertal, Germany, and was previously Professor at Hamburg University of Fine Arts (1965–76) and the University of Applied Arts, Vienna (1977–80). In 1992 he was awarded an honorary doctorate at ETH (Swiss Federal Institute for Technology, Zurich) and in 2012 at the Hochschule für Gestaltung Karlsruhe. Between 1968 and 1992 he led the documenta schools for visitors. He currently runs courses for "professional citizens" at the Karlsruhe University of Arts and Design (Rector: Peter Sloterdijk). He is a member of the Institut für theoretische Kunst, Universalpoesie und Prognostik and founder of the Amt für Arbeit an unlösbaren Problemen und Maßnahmen der hohen Hand, Berlin.

Prof. Saul David, Ph.D. is Professor of War Studies at the University of Buckingham and Course Director and Tutor of Buckingham's London-based MA in Military History by Research, "The Art of War from

Napoleon to Iraq, 1793–2003." Professor David received a history MA from the University of Edinburgh and a history Ph.D. from the University of Glasgow where his doctoral research focused on the Bengal Army and the origins of the Indian Mutiny of 1857. He specializes in the history of the British Army and the Wars of Empire and his many publications include *The Indian Mutiny* (Penguin, 2002, shortlisted for the Westminster Medal for Military Literature), *Zulu: The Tragedy and Heroism of the Zulu War of 1879* (Penguin, 2004), *Victoria's Wars: Rise of Empire* (Penguin, 2006), and *All the King's Men: The British Soldier from the Restoration to Waterloo* (Penguin, 2012). He has recently been working on a history of World War I: *100 Days to Victory: How the First World War Was Won*, was published by Hodder & Stoughton in 2013.

Professor David is an experienced broadcaster and regularly presents and appears in history programs on British TV and radio. In 2012 he appeared on BBC Radio 4's *In Our Time* discussion about Clausewitz and *On War*.

Dr. Corinne Michaela Flick studied both law and literature, taking American studies as her subsidiary. She gained her Dr. Phil. in 1989. She has worked as in-house lawyer for Bertelsmann Buch AG and Amazon.com. In 1998 she became General Partner in

Vivil GmbH und Co. KG, Offenburg. She is Founder and Chair of the Convoco Foundation.

Dr. Flick is Chair of the Board of Trustees of the Aspen Institute, Germany; member of the board of the Alfred Herrhausen Society—The international Forum of Deutsche Bank; member of the board of the Osterfestspiele Salzburg; and a member of the Executive Committee of the International Council of the Tate Gallery, London.

Prof. Dr. Gerd Gigerenzer gained his Dr. Phil. in psychology in 1977 and his postdoctoral qualification in psychology in 1982 from Munich University. Since 1997 he has been Director at the Max Planck Institute for Human Development and Director of the Harding Center for Risk Literacy in Berlin since its inception in 2009. He is former Professor of Psychology at the University of Chicago and John M. Olin Distinguished Visiting Professor, School of Law at the University of Virginia. He is also Batten Fellow at the Darden Business School, University of Virginia, and Fellow of the Berlin-Brandenburg Academy of Sciences and the German Academy of Sciences. Awards for his work include the AAAS Prize for the best article in the behavioral sciences and the Association of American Publishers Prize for the best book in the social and behavioral sciences. His award-winning popular books, *Calculated Risks: How to Know When Numbers Deceive You* (2002) and *Gut Feelings: The Intelligence of the Unconscious* (2008), have been translated into eighteen languages. In his latest book, *Risk Savvy: How to Make Good Decisions* (2014), he discusses how to deal effectively with risk. His research interests include bounded rationality and social intelligence; decisions under uncertainty and time restrictions; competence in risk and risk communication; decision-making strategies of managers, judges, and physicians.

Prof. Dr. Dr. h.c. mult. Paul Kirchhof gained his Ph.D. Dr. jur. in 1968 and his postdoctoral qualification in 1974. From 1975 to 1981 he was Professor of Public Law and Tax Law in Münster. Since 1981 he has been Professor of Public Law and Tax Law in Heidelberg. From 1987 to 1999 he was a Judge of the Federal Constitutional Court of Germany. Since April 2013 he has been President of the Heidelberg Academy of Sciences and Humanities. Professor Kirchhof's publications on constitutional, administrative and tax law include *Besteuerungsgewalt und Grundgesetz* (1973), *Verwalten durch mittelbares Einwirken* (1976), *Die kulturellen Voraussetzungen der Freiheit* (1995), *Der sanfte Verlust der Freiheit. Für ein* *neues Steuerrecht* (2004), *Das Gesetz der Hydra* (2006), *Das Mass der Gerechtigkeit—Bringt unser Land wieders ins Gleichgewicht!* (2009), and *Deutschland im Schuldensog. Der Weg vom Bürgen zurück zum Bürger* (2013).

Prof. Dr. Kai A. Konrad gained his doctorate (1990) and his postdoctoral qualification (1993) at the University of Munich. He has taught and undertaken research at the Universities of Munich, Bonn, Bergen (Norway), and the University of California, Irvine. From 1994 to 2009 he was Professor of Economics at the Free University, Berlin, and from 2001 to 2009 he was Director of the Social Science Research Center, Berlin. Since January 2011 he has been Director at the Max Planck Institute for Tax Law and Public Finance. He is co-editor of the *Journal of Public Economics*, and serves on the editorial board of a number of other international academic journals. He is author of more than eighty articles in international economic and political journals. He is Chairman of the Council of Scientific Advisors to the German Ministry of Finance.

Prof. Dr. Stefan Korioth gained his doctorate in law in 1990 and completed his postdoctoral qualification in public and constitutional law. From 1996 to 2000 he was Professor of Public Law, Constitutional History, and Theory of Government at Greifswald. In 2000 he accepted the Chair of Public and Ecclesiastical Law at LMU, Munich. His publications include *Integration und Bundesstaat* (1990), *Der Finanzausgleich zwischen Bund und Ländern* (1997), *Grundzüge des Staatskirchenrechts* (with B. Jean d'Heur, 2000), and *Das Bundesverfassungsgericht* (with Klaus Schlaich, ninth edition, 2012).

Prof. Dr. Christoph G. Paulus studied law at Munich, taking his doctorate in law in 1980. His postdoctoral qualification, gained in 1991, was in civil law, civil procedure and Roman law, for which he was awarded the Medal of the University of Paris II. He received his LL.M at Berkeley in 1983–4 and returned to Berkeley from 1989 to 1990 as a recipient of a Feodor Lynen Stipend from the Humboldt Foundation. In 1992–4 he was Associate Professor at Augsburg, and from the summer semester 1994 he was at the Law Faculty of the Humboldt University in Berlin, becoming Dean of the Faculty in 2008–10. In 2009 he was made Director of the Research Center Institute for Interdisciplinary Restructuring, and Consultant to the International Monetary Fund and the

World Bank. Among other roles he is Member (and Director) of the International Insolvency Institute of the American College of Bankruptcy and the International Association for Procedural Law. Since 2006 he has been advisor on insolvency law to the German delegation to UNCITRAL. He is on the editorial board of the *Zeitschrift für Wirtschaftsrecht* (ZIP), the *Norton Annual Review of International Insolvency*, and the *International Insolvency Law Review*, among other journals.

Prof. Jörg Rocholl, Ph.D. is president of ESMT European School of Management and Technology in Berlin and holds the Ernst & Young Chair in Governance and Compliance. Professor Rocholl graduated from the Universität Witten/Herdecke, where he earned a degree in economics (with honors). After completing his Ph.D. at Columbia University in New York, he was named an assistant professor at the University of North Carolina at Chapel Hill. Professor Rocholl has researched and taught at ESMT since 2007 and was appointed President of ESMT in 2011. He is a member of the economic advisory board of the German Federal Ministry of Finance, Research Professor at the Ifo Institute in Munich and Duisenberg, and Fellow of the European Central Bank (ECB).

Prof. Dr. Burkhard Schwenker was Chairman of the Executive Committee of Roland Berger Strategy Consultants between 2003 and 2010, when he became Chairman of the Supervisory Board until he was re-elected CEO in May 2013. After studying business administration and mathematics, he started his career at PWA Papierwerke Waldhof-Aschaffenburg AG. In 1989 he completed his Ph.D. and joined Roland Berger Strategy Consultants the same year. He was elected Partner in 1992. He is an expert in strategy, organization, and corporate transformation. Burkhard Schwenker teaches strategic management at the Leipzig Graduate School of Management (HHL), where he is also Academic Co-Director of the HHL's Center for Scenario Planning. He sits on the Board of the German Academic Association for Business Research, is a member of the University Council at the Technical University Bergakademie Freiberg, and serves on the Board of Trustees of several universities. Burkhard Schwenker is Visiting Fellow at the Saïd Business School, University of Oxford. In February 2012, Burkhard Schwenker was appointed Chairman of the Roland Berger School of Strategy and Economics (RBSE). In addition to his professional and academic work, Burkhard Schwenker takes an active role in several sociopolitical institutions and foundations. For instance, he is Chairman of the Roland Berger Foundation's Board of Trustees, Deputy Chairman of Atlantik Brücke e.V., Chairman of the Board of the Hamburg Symphony Orchestra, and a member of the Senate or Board of Trustees for among others the Wertekommission—Initiative wertebewusste Führung (Values Commission for the Initiative on Values-Based Management), the Stiftung Initiative Wertestipendium (Foundation for the Values Stipend Foundation) and the World Wide Fund for Nature (WWF).

www.ingramcontent.com/pod-product-compliance
Lightning Source LLC
Chambersburg PA
CBHW060042030426
42334CB00019B/2446